THE HEALTH OF THE NATION

The Irish Healthcare
System 1957–2007

THE HEALTH OF THE NATION

The Irish Healthcare
System 1957–2007

PADRAIG O'MORAIN

Gill & Macmillan

Gill & Macmillan Ltd
Hume Avenue, Park West, Dublin 12
with associated companies throughout the world
www.gillmacmillan.ie

© Vhi Healthcare 2007
978 07171 4184 5
Index compiled by Helen Litton
Type design by Make Communication
Typesetting and print origination by Carrigboy Typesetting Services
Printed and bound in Great Britain by MPG Books Ltd, Bodmin, Cornwall

This book is typeset in Minion 13pt/16pt.

The paper used in this book comes from the wood pulp
of managed forests. For every tree felled, at least one tree
is planted, thereby renewing natural resources.

A CIP catalogue record is available for this book
from the British Library.

5 4 3 2 1

CONTENTS

This book was commissioned by Vhi Healthcare
to mark its 50th anniversary in 2007.

'For 50 years, when you've needed us—we've been there.'

PART ONE

Chapter 1 ～

OVERVIEW AND SUMMARY

INTRODUCTION

This chapter provides a quick reference guide to the history of the health services as outlined in the rest of the book. Of necessity, it omits much of the detail and context which can be found in the other chapters. Beside each heading is given the number of the chapter in which more information can be found. *Sources are fully acknowledged in the individual chapters.*

HOSPITALS—EXPANSION, CONTRACTION AND RESISTANCE (CHAPTER 2)

The Irish hospital system comprises three distinct types of hospitals. These are public, voluntary and private.

The public hospitals by and large began their existence as workhouses or infirmaries in the 19th century. The oldest hospitals in the country are the voluntary hospitals established largely by charities and later by religious orders. They are almost entirely reliant on public funding.

The public hospital system also includes long-stay hospitals, both public and voluntary. Specialist hospitals treating cancer, tuberculosis, other infectious diseases, and orthopaedic complaints were established mainly as voluntary hospitals.

Historically, private hospitals have been few in number though new policy developments suggest this is about to change.

The Hospitals Commission was the first of a number of bodies established to advise on the funding of the hospital system. In its report in 1936 it proposed a rationalisation of hospitals which was rejected.

The Fitzgerald Report, produced by a consultative council in 1967, recommended that the country should be served by four regional hospitals, each with 600–1,000 beds. In addition, there would be nine general hospitals each of which would have a minimum of 300 beds. County hospitals would, in some cases, become general hospitals and in other cases become akin to district hospitals in their role and staffing.

These proposals were seen by the supporters of county hospitals as a threat to their viability, and the recommendations were never implemented.

With the economy in serious trouble, the 1980s ushered in more than a decade of spending restrictions and cutbacks. These 'rationalised' hospital services in a more crude way than anybody had envisaged.

Thousands of hospital beds were removed from the system. Between 1984 and 1993 as many as 6,000 beds were closed.

As the population grew and the economy boomed in the 1990s, the demand on hospital services increased and it quickly became clear that the hospitals were unable to meet these demands.

The decade began with the extension of an entitlement to free hospital service to the entire population in 1991. But, as Curry (2003) points out, the waiting list for planned surgical and other procedures remained at an average of about 30,000 throughout the decade.

Also a major source of dissatisfaction were reports of major delays in Accident and Emergency departments.

It was partly in response to these complaints that the government published its *Quality and Fairness, A Health System for You* in November 2001. The health strategy promised the provision of 3,000 extra public beds by 2011. It also promised that nobody would wait more than three months for a planned procedure once they had seen a consultant. The National Treatment Purchase Fund was set up in 2002 to purchase treatment for public patients in private hospitals.

In 2002, the Minister for Health, Micheál Martin TD, established a task force to recommend how the *European Working Time Directive* which, from August 2004, limited the working week of non-consultant hospital doctors, could be implemented in the hospital system.

The report—known as the Hanly Report—suggested that acute hospital services should be reorganised on a population basis. Each population of about 350,000 people would be served by a network of hospitals with a regional hospital at the centre. The smaller hospitals, particularly the county hospitals would no longer be acute hospitals but would provide outpatient clinics and would have convalescent beds and small injuries clinics.

As happened in the case of the Fitzgerald Report, Hanly's recommended reorganisation was seen as a downgrading of the county hospital. A well-organised opposition to the suggestions emerged. However, the secretary general of the Department of Health, Mr Michael Scanlan, told the Dáil Public Accounts Committee in October 2005 that the implementation of the Hanly reforms remained on his agenda.

For most of the period covered by this book private hospitals have played a relatively modest role in the Irish hospital system. However, as the period came to an end there were strong indications that this might be about to change.

In the 1990s, tax incentives were introduced in the Finance Bill to encourage the development of new private hospitals. The private hospital sector received a further boost in 2005, when the Minister for Health, Mary Harney TD, announced a policy of encouraging the private sector to build private hospitals on the same campuses as public hospitals.

CARE IN THE COMMUNITY—COMMUNITY CARE AND PRIMARY CARE (CHAPTER 3)

For more than a century, community healthcare as provided by the State was based largely on the dispensary system and on measures to reduce the incidence and spread of infectious diseases.

Under the dispensary system, which persisted until 1972, each district employed a salaried doctor to provide free medical care to the poor of the area.

The dispensary system was brought to an end by the Health Act, 1970.

Under the Choice of Doctor General Medical Services Scheme, which replaced the dispensary system, persons whose income was below a certain limit were entitled to free consultations with the GP of their choice and to free prescribed medicines.

The GP Visit Card was introduced in 2005. The card entitles persons whose means exceed the guidelines for the Medical Card to see their GP free of charge.

However, unlike the Medical Card, the GP Visit Card does not cover the cost of prescribed medicines.

The 2001 health strategy outlined a vision of primary care in which the provision of services in the community would become the core of the health service generally. This section of the strategy was published separately under the title *Primary Care: A New Direction*.

Services would be provided by primary care teams which would include not only doctors and nurses but also healthcare assistants, home helps, physiotherapists, occupational therapists, social workers and administrative personnel.

Patients who attended dispensaries, up to 1972, were usually supplied with medicines by the dispensary doctors themselves. Under the new Choice of Doctor Scheme, patients received their prescribed medicines free of charge from retail pharmacists.

The Health Act, 1970, also provided for free prescribed drugs for persons with certain long-term ailments. This eventually became the Long-Term Illness Scheme. Sixteen conditions are covered by the scheme.

A scheme to enable people who did not qualify for medical cards to recoup part of the cost of prescribed drugs was introduced in 1971. It has evolved into the current Drugs Payments Scheme.

A scheme to enable VHI members to recoup the cost of prescribed drugs and medicines was introduced in 1967. It was discontinued when the organisation cut costs to deal with losses in the late 1980s.[1]

Prior to the 1970s, older people unable to care for themselves, and who did not have a family able or willing to care for them, were accommodated in County Homes. These County Homes, in many cases, had previously been workhouses and conditions tended to be very poor.

This state of affairs continued until 1968 when the *Care of the Aged* report was published. The report advocated that, as a matter of policy, older people should be enabled to live in their own homes for as long as possible.

The report strongly influenced government policy (Coakley, 1997). Social welfare benefits were improved. The County Homes were replaced by Welfare Homes. Sheltered housing was built.

Financial schemes to enable older people to live at home, such as grants for house repairs, were introduced.

However, a subsequent report, *The Years Ahead: Policy for the Elderly* (1988), found that the situation remained unsatisfactory.

The report suggested the development of rehabilitation and day care services to enable people to live in their own communities for longer.

Special care teams and coordinators of services were appointed to community care districts and more community hospitals were developed. However, Coakley (1997) points out that these developments have been patchy.

A Carer's Allowance was introduced in 1990.

The 2001 health strategy recommended that services be brought to an adequate level over a 10-year period through a number of measures including additional day centre places.

The Community Protection Programme refers in particular to measures to protect the public against infectious diseases. The control of infectious diseases is one of the success stories of the health services. Among the successes of the programme was the elimination of tuberculosis as a major health issue.

Immunisation programmes have also reduced diseases such as smallpox, diphtheria, polio and German measles (rubella) to the point where they are no longer a source of fear or of significant levels of ill health.

Public health nursing was originally developed on a voluntary basis. The development of a public health nursing service by the State began in the 1950s.

Part of the work of the health administration services has been the payment of certain cash benefits. These include allowances related to disability and illness and also the Supplementary Welfare Allowance.

MENTAL HEALTH CARE—FROM THE INSTITUTION TO THE COMMUNITY (CHAPTER 4)

In the 19th century, persons who were mentally ill may have formed the biggest single group of people being 'cared for' by the health services. They were incarcerated in asylums which provided neither nursing nor adequate treatment. Many asylums later became mental hospitals.

The asylums and psychiatric hospitals had a significant economic impact. In 1951, patients in the asylum accounted for almost half the population of Ballinasloe, Co. Galway (Walsh, 1997). Full-time employees accounted for about a fifth of those townspeople who were not mental patients.

The 1945 Mental Treatment Act introduced the designation of categories of patients as voluntary or temporary. Previously, the law had simply assumed that patients with psychiatric illnesses would not willingly go to hospital and all admissions were involuntary.

The psychiatric hospitals were a substitute for the provision of appropriate services elsewhere for other groups as well. By 1963, as many as 16% of people living in psychiatric hospitals were not mentally ill but had learning difficulties or other intellectual disabilities. The population of mental hospitals also included unmarried mothers and children (Ferriter, 2004).

Conditions were bad, with some hospital wards containing as many as 120 patients. Not only were conditions poor but Ireland had more psychiatric in-patients than any other country in the world—a fact which the World Health Organisation commented on in the early 1960s (Ferriter, 2004).

The *Report of the Commission of Inquiry on Mental Illness*, published in 1966, recommended that the big psychiatric hospitals gradually be replaced with psychiatric units attached to general hospitals and that care be provided in the community where possible.

Ardkeen Hospital in Waterford opened the first psychiatric unit in a general hospital in 1965. Some out-patient clinics were developed. Sanatoria, no longer needed for TB patients, were, in a number of cases, turned over to the psychiatric services.

In Dublin, the Eastern Health Board established mental health services on a geographical basis with each local service headed by a clinical director.

However, no plan was ever drawn up to implement the Commission's report in a cohesive way.

In 1981, the Minister for Health, Eileen Desmond TD, established a study group which, three years later, produced the report *Planning for the Future.*

Planning for the Future envisaged that services would be provided on a localised basis: as far as was possible, people with psychiatric illnesses would be treated in a community setting;

existing long-stay patients would be rehabilitated so that they too could live in the community; a psychiatry of old age would be developed; services for alcoholics would be locally based in the community; other drug problems would also be dealt with in the community; and children's psychiatric services would be developed and extended to the whole country.

Localised services were set up in most areas and a slow but steady process of providing psychiatric units in general hospitals was undertaken.

By the late 1990s, it had become the norm for mental health patients to be seen at facilities located in the community rather than in psychiatric hospitals.

The passing of the Mental Health Act, 2001, led to the establishment of the Mental Health Commission, the creation of a new Inspectorate of Mental Health Services (replacing the Inspector of Mental Hospitals), and the setting up of mental health review boards to consider the case of every person involuntarily detained in a psychiatric hospital.

The Mental Health Commission, established in 2002, is the agency mainly responsible for vindicating the rights of psychiatric patients and for promoting quality in the delivery of mental health services.

In 2006, *A Vision for Change*, a new strategy for the mental health services, was published by the Department of Health and Children. It recommended that the State's fifteen public psychiatric hospitals should be closed over a period of ten years and the money raised should be used to fund services in the community.

Recent years have seen a growth in the availability and use of counselling. In its directory for 2005–2007, the Irish Association for Counselling and Psychotherapy listed almost 1,000 accredited counsellors who had undergone specified forms of training.

A range of services, ranging from self-help to training, are provided by non-governmental organisations. The more prominent include Schizophrenia Ireland, Mental Health Ireland, Aware, GROW and Recovery Inc.

THE HEALTH SERVICES AND DISABILITY (CHAPTER 5)

Until comparatively recently, people with disabilities were hidden away in hospitals, psychiatric and otherwise. To have a disability was to be excluded from society.

With the exception of psychiatric patients, persons with intellectual disabilities were more marginalised than any other disabled group half a century ago.

Even children as young as seven were admitted to adult psychiatric hospitals.

The 1950s saw the establishment of parents' organisations aimed at enabling their intellectually-disabled children to live at home while attending special schools.

In the 1980s and the 1990s, a policy to move persons with intellectual disabilities out of psychiatric hospitals and into more suitable facilities was under way.

It was only in the 1980s that the issue of services for people with disabilities and of their status in society began to be discussed in a consistent way.

When the health boards were established under the Health Act, 1970, responsibility for disability services was given to each board's Special Hospital Care Programme.

By the 1990s, the policy and attitudes towards the position of people with disabilities had firmly changed. The goal now was to enable persons with disabilities to live as independently as possible, preferably in their own homes in the community, and to take as complete a role in the activities of society as was possible.

The review group report, *Towards an Independent Future*, published in 1996, emphasised the view that people with disabilities should be enabled to live as independently as possible.

The Commission on the Status of People with Disabilities was established by the government in 1993. In drawing 60% of its membership from among service users, the Commission exemplified the new way of thinking about disability.

Its report was wide-ranging but perhaps the most important principle put forward was that services for persons with disabilities should be mainstreamed.

This meant that services for disabled people would be provided by the same organisations that provide a service for everybody else. Thus, for instance, the training and employment authority FÁS has taken over certain functions of the National Rehabilitation Board.

The Council for the Status of People with Disabilities was established in 1997. It is now known as People with Disabilities in Ireland. Its objective was to be an official body representative of persons with disabilities.

A Department of Equality and Law Reform was set up in 1997, though it was later subsumed into the Department of Justice, Equality and Law Reform. That Department's Disability Equality Section provides a focal point for disability equality policy and legislation development.

The Forum of People with Disabilities, a non-governmental organisation, lobbies and advocates on behalf of people with disabilities. It strongly influenced the establishment of the Commission on the Status of People with Disabilities. It also effectively secured the creation of the permanent Council for the Status of People with Disabilities (now People with Disabilities in Ireland).

Two new structures to promote the interests of people with disabilities were set up in 2000.

The National Disability Authority was established to promote and secure the rights of people with disabilities.

People with Disabilities in Ireland (PDI) was established with funding from the Department of Justice, Equality and Law Reform as a successor to the Council for the Status of People with Disabilities. Its role is to bring together people with disabilities both nationally and locally to influence decision-making about issues that have an impact on their lives.

By 2006 there were, according to an estimate by PDI, almost 400,000 people in Ireland with disabilities of one kind or another—roughly 10% of the population.

The Citizens Information Board (formerly Comhairle), the national agency responsible for supporting the provision of information, advice and advocacy on social services, has been given the task, under the Comhairle Act, 2000, of developing advocacy services which will enable people with disabilities to obtain their entitlements.

The Disability Act, 2005, when fully implemented, will entitle disabled persons to obtain from the Health Service Executive a statement of their needs and a plan for the provision of these needs. The implementation of the Act is to be phased in by the end of 2011.

It remains the case, though, that to have a disability is to be severely disadvantaged. In 2005, as many as 13,076 people were still waiting for an assessment for therapeutic intervention and rehabilitation services, according to the Health Research Board's analysis of the National Physical and Sensory Disability Database.

FROM COUNTY COUNCIL TO HEALTH SERVICE EXECUTIVE—THE EVOLUTION OF HEALTH ADMINISTRATION (CHAPTER 6)

The 19th century saw the introduction of the rudiments of a health service which continued into comparatively recent times. For instance, a dispensary system was introduced under the Poor Relief Act, 1851. The country was divided into dispensary districts and a doctor was employed in each district to provide a free service to poor people in the locality.

A Department of Local Government and Public Health was established by the Ministers and Secretaries Act, 1924. The Department of Health was established in 1947.

The funding of health services shifted from local taxation (rates) to central government between the 1940s and the late 1970s.

The administration of health services at local level was undertaken by county councils and county boroughs until 1971. Mental hospitals were governed by special joint boards.

The 27 health authorities which had administered health services locally were replaced by eight regional health boards from 1 April 1971. The work of the health boards was organised in three 'programmes': community care, general hospitals and special hospitals i.e. services for persons with mental illness and other disabilities.

The dispensary system was replaced by the Choice of Doctor Scheme in 1972. Under the scheme, persons who passed a means test, and certain other categories of people, became entitled to a free General Practitioner service, free prescribed medicines and a free public ward hospital service.

Following the implementation of changes brought about by the Health Act, 1970, a series of reports and government strategies paved the way for further developments. They included:

The Commission on Health Funding, 1989
The Commission recommended that the Department of Health become a policy-making body and disengage from managing health services and that the health boards should be replaced by a Health Services Executive Authority.

Planning for the Future, 1984
The report recommended that psychiatric institutions be replaced with psychiatric wards in general hospitals and that community-based services be improved and developed.

Shaping a Healthier Future, 1994
The 1994 Health Strategy recommended that health planners should focus on achieving positive outcomes for patients and not just on the level of service or the amount of services provided.

The Health Strategy, Quality and Fairness, A Health System for You

Quality and Fairness, A Health System for You envisaged the provision of 3,000 extra public beds by 2011. It provided for the establishment of the National Treatment Purchase Fund to pay for public patients to be treated in private hospitals in Ireland and in the UK. It envisaged an expansion and development of GP services. It envisaged the establishment of a Health Service Executive.

Mental Health Act, 2001

The Mental Health Act, 2001, led to the establishment of the Mental Health Commission which has two roles: to protect the rights of psychiatric patients and to ensure that high-quality care is provided by the psychiatric services.

Other developments

In 2000, the Eastern Regional Health Authority replaced the former Eastern Health Board. Three Area Health Boards were established within the ERHA region. These were the East Coast Area Health Board, the Northern Area Health Board and the South Western Area Health Board.

Health Service Executive

The Health Service Executive replaced the regional health boards and the Eastern Regional Health Authority in January 2005. It is made up of the National Hospitals Office which administers hospital services nationally, the Primary Community and Continuing Care Directorate which has responsibility for non-hospital services in the community and the National Shared Services Centre which is responsible for payroll, personnel and similar functions.

Private healthcare

Public involvement in the administration of private health has been more in the nature of indirect influence than direct involvement. There has been no unified system of administration of private hospitals. In recent years, however, the involvement of the State in private healthcare has increased. The major example of this is the National Treatment Purchase Fund.

THE MEDICAL AND NURSING PROFESSIONS (CHAPTER 7)

Doctors

At the start of the 20th century, voluntary hospitals, mainly in Dublin, provided a free service for the very poor. Local authority hospitals had their origins in the infirmaries attached to workhouses and the standard of care often reflected this. For the poor, a GP service was provided from district dispensaries. This was the context within which doctors worked.

The Irish Medical Association, like its counterpart the British Medical Association, was founded in the 1830s. Its main focus was on dispensary doctors. The members of the British Medical Association in Ireland tended to be specialists or other doctors in private practice.

The Local Government Act, 1925, provided for the appointment of Medical Officers of Health to oversee public health measures.

The Fianna Fáil government elected in 1932 appointed Dr F.C. Ward TD as Parliamentary Secretary to the Minister for Local Government and Public Health. Dr Ward expanded public health measures including school medical examinations and increased the number of public hospitals.

In 1944 Dr James Deeny, a GP, was appointed Chief Medical Officer. He can take much of the credit for ending the scourge of TB as a devastating illness. Deeny invested in sanatoria and provided for the employment of more thoracic surgeons and other professionals.

In 1946, the Minister for Health, Seán MacEntee TD, put forward a plan which, if implemented, would make a free GP service available to about 75% of the population. The Irish Medical Association opposed the plan on the grounds that a state medical service would be a breach of the moral law. The IMA also opposed a plan to provide a free health service to mothers and their children up to the age of sixteen, the Mother and Child Scheme.

In 1948, Fianna Fáil was defeated in a general election and a coalition government, led by Fine Gael which opposed the extension of free medical services, took power. Dr Noel Browne TD was appointed Minister for Health.

Dr Browne's abrasive personality worsened relations with the IMA and the Catholic hierarchy which also opposed the Mother and Child Scheme. The cabinet was not prepared to oppose the bishops and Browne resigned.

In the subsequent general election, Fianna Fáil returned to power and successfully set about preparing the 1953 Health Act which provided for a scaled-down Mother and Child Scheme and an extension of eligibility for free hospital services to most of the population.

The Minister, Dr James Ryan, was more diplomatic than Dr Browne in his dealings with the IMA, seeking its views on how the health services might be improved.

He was succeeded by T.F. O'Higgins who, in talks with the IMA, agreed to set up an advisory body which led to the establishment of the Voluntary Health Insurance Board in 1957.

After Mr Seán MacEntee became Minister for Health in 1957 he refused to accept the Irish Medical Association as a negotiator under the Trade Union Act, 1941. In 1963 it was agreed that an Irish Medical Union would be set up to negotiate pay and conditions. In 1984, the IMA and the IMU were amalgamated to form the Irish Medical Organisation with trade union negotiating rights.

In 1972, the dispensaries were replaced by the Choice of Doctor Scheme.

A government attempt to provide an entitlement to free hospital services to all from 1974 was successfully opposed by consultants who believed such a move would have an adverse effect on their income and conditions of employment (Curry, 2003).[2] Eligibility for hospital services was broadened to most of the population in 1979 and to all in 1991.

A consultants' contract, negotiated in 1981, gave consultants employment as pensionable public servants with a requirement that they work 33 hours per week. It also gave them a right to unlimited private practice.

The IMO represents registered medical practitioners in all areas of work. The Irish Hospital Consultants Association represents most consultants.

The Medical Council was formed following the passing of the Medical Practitioners Act in 1978.

Nurses
The 19th century brought the establishment of hospitals by nuns who saw nursing the poor as a religious vocation. Their standards were high, as were those of the lay voluntary hospitals influenced by the ideas of Florence Nightingale.

The training of nurses was through an apprenticeship system in which the young nurses learned from senior nurses in a system requiring strict obedience.

Psychiatric hospitals employed attendants, male and female, rather than nurses. The replacement of attendants by fully-trained psychiatric nurses was not completed in the psychiatric hospitals until the 1960s.

Public health nursing was provided largely on a voluntary basis.

Midwifery began to be regulated through the Midwives (Ireland) Act, 1918. General nursing was first regulated by the Nurses

Registration (Ireland) Act, 1919. The regulation of nurses was taken over by An Bord Altranais (The Nursing Board) in 1951 when it was established under the Nurses Act, 1950.

In 1919, the Irish Nurses Union was formed as part of the Irish Women Workers Union. The Irish Nurses Organisation evolved from the Irish Nurses Union in 1949. Nurses are also organised by SIPTU, IMPACT and the Psychiatric Nurses Association. A nurses' strike took place in 1999.

The first Nursing Adviser was appointed to the Department of Health in 1949. The development of community and public health nursing was provided for in the Health Acts of 1947 and 1953.

The Commission on Nursing was established in 1997 and its work led to a modernising of the profession of nursing both in terms of management and of clinical practice.

Nurse training became a degree course from the 2002/2003 academic year, thus bringing an end to the old apprenticeship system.

The Irish Medicines Board (Miscellaneous Provisions) Act, 2006, provides for authority to be given to nurses to prescribe certain medicines.

FINANCING THE HEALTH SYSTEM (CHAPTER 8)

From the late 19th century and until 1947, the cost of the public health services was borne almost entirely by local authorities which derived their funding from local ratepayers.

Voluntary hospitals funded out of philanthropic donations were set up mainly in Dublin in the 19th century.

The Hospitals Trust Fund provided a substantial boost to the development of hospitals. The Fund was financed by sweepstakes on horse races and became a major source of capital funding for public hospitals. The sweepstakes continued until the early 1980s.

In 1947, State grants met only 16% of the cost of providing health services. The remainder was raised by ratepayers. Under

the Health Services (Financial Provisions) Act, the maximum contribution by the local authorities was limited to the equivalent of
their contribution in the year ending March 1948, plus half of any
amount over that. The remainder would be paid by the Exchequer.

Part-financing of the health services out of local taxation
ended in 1977.

By the end of the period covered by this book, almost the entire
cost of the public health services was being met by the Exchequer.

The 1980s was a period of cutbacks and spending restraints in
the health services due to concern over the national debt.
Spending on health, which had stood at 7.72% of Gross Domestic
Product in 1980, had been pared back to 7.04% by 1985. Deep cuts
from 1987 reduced the proportion again to 5.72% in 1990.

Between the end of 1983 and the end of 1989, the number of
beds was reduced by 22%.

Economic growth in the mid-1990s brought increased health
spending which had risen to 7.39% of GDP by 2002.

The lion's share of the revenue allocation for health services
went to general hospitals. By the end of the period they were
receiving about half of all expenditure while community care
received between a quarter and one third of expenditure.

The Commission on Health Funding, established in 1987 at
a time of cutbacks in health spending, concluded that the
difficulties in the health services owed more to the way these
services were organised than to funding.[3]

Questions of funding and of equity of access to health services
by public patients continued to loom large in public debate, and
an audit of the value for money provided by the health service
was commissioned by the Department of Health and Children.

The report, *Value for Money Audit of the Irish Health System*
(2001), identified problems which arose from the underfunding of
services in the 1980s.[4] Its authors saw the growing demand for
healthcare and the growing cost of that care as the fundamental
problem facing the health services.

The 2001 health strategy addressed the issue of access. Access would be improved, it suggested, by a number of measures: 3,000 public hospital beds would be added to the system; more hospital consultants would be employed; and any adult waiting longer than three months for hospital treatment would be provided with private treatment by the National Treatment Purchase Fund.

The National Treatment Purchase Fund arranges treatment, free of charge, for those public patients who have been longest on the waiting list. Treatment is provided in private hospitals in Ireland and the UK. The first treatments under the NTPF were carried out in 2002. By April 2006, a total of 42,000 people had been treated.

In 2004, the NTPF was also assigned the role of compiling hospital waiting lists because of inaccuracies in the traditional waiting lists. By April 2006, the Patient Treatment Register covered nineteen hospitals and 74% of historical waiting list data.

Wiley (1997) notes that the public component of health expenditure fell from 85% in the 1980s to 75% in the mid-1990s. The other 25%, she states, is accounted for by the private sector. This is made up of health insurance companies, general practitioners, pharmacists and private hospitals.[5]

Eligibility for services
In 1957, when the VHI was established, entitlement to public hospital services was income-based in a three-tier system. Those on the lowest incomes were entitled to free hospital treatment, those on the highest incomes (about 15% of the population) had no entitlement and the middle group had some entitlement to free or subsidised treatment.

The Health Act, 1970, continued the three-tier system.

In 1979, the right to free hospital maintenance and treatment was extended to all except a group made up of persons on the highest incomes.

In 1991, the entitlement to free hospital maintenance and treatment as public patients was extended to all, regardless of income.

CONTROVERSY AND SCANDAL (CHAPTER 9)
Introduction
Clashes of ideology, self-interest, and individual and systemic failings all play their part in how the health services work—or fail to work—and in how they are shaped.

In recent decades, scandals in the health system have ended the era of unquestioning acceptance of the views of doctors or of bodies administering health services.

What follows here is mention of some of the more significant of controversies and scandals of the period.

Contraception
In response to Catholic Church lobbying, the Censorship of Publications Act, 1929, banned the publication of information on contraception and abortion. In 1935, the Criminal Law (Amendment) Act banned the importation and sale of contraceptives.

Nevertheless, in 1969 a fertility guidance clinic was opened in Dublin with the support of the Family Planning Rights Group and of the International Planned Parenthood Association.

In 1973, the Supreme Court in *McGee vs Attorney General* found that married couples were entitled to obtain contraceptives for their personal use.

The Health (Family Planning) Act, 1979, allowed GPs to prescribe contraceptives for medical reasons or for *bona fide* family planning purposes.

The restrictions introduced by the 1979 Act were removed in 1985 by amendments allowing condoms to be sold freely to persons aged eighteen or more. In 1993 the Health (Family Planning) Amendment Act placed an obligation on health boards to provide family planning services.

Blood products

The Blood Transfusion Service Board was involved in three scandals concerning blood and blood products:

Haemophiliacs

It emerged in the 1980s that a blood product called Factor VIII, imported by the BTSB from the United States and given to haemophiliacs, had infected more than half the 400 haemophiliacs in the Republic with HIV or Hepatitis C, and in some cases with both.

Anti-D

It emerged in the 1990s that more than 1,000 women had been infected with Hepatitis C by Anti-D immunoglobulin treatment using a blood product provided by the BTSB.

Notification delay

It emerged during the course of the Finlay Tribunal into the Anti-D scandal that there had been a delay of, in some cases, months and in others of years in informing 28 blood donors that they had tested positive for Hepatitis C antibodies.

Organ retention

Controversy over the retention of organs following post-mortems, especially of children, arose in 1999, following the exposure of similar practices in Britain. A report (2006) by Dr Deirdre Madden, based on evidence collected by the Dunne Inquiry, found that doctors believed they were sparing the feelings of parents by not telling them that their children's organs might be retained. This was the practice not only in Ireland but in other countries and doctors should be judged by the standards which prevailed at that time.

Hysterectomies—the Neary case

In 1990, two midwives at Our Lady of Lourdes Hospital in Drogheda expressed concerns to the North Eastern Health Board about the level of hysterectomies being carried out there by consultant obstetrician Dr Michael Neary. It emerged later that Dr Neary had carried out 129 peripartum hysterectomies between 1974 and 1998. The majority of obstetricians carry out fewer than ten such hysterectomies in their careers. Dr Neary was removed from the medical register in 2003.

A report into the affair by Judge Maureen Harding Clarke found that nobody at the hospital or no institution dealing with the hospital raised concerns about Dr Neary's activities until the two midwives spoke to the North Eastern Health Board which had taken over the hospital from the Medical Missionaries of Mary.

A compensation scheme for women affected by Dr Neary's activities was announced by the government in 2007.

MRSA

Hospital-based infections such as MRSA (Methicillin-Resistant Staphylococcus Aureus), particularly following surgery, became a major issue from 2000 onwards.

The Minister for Health and Children, Mary Harney TD, told the Dáil in October 2006 that the spread of MRSA was caused mainly by over-prescribing of antibiotics though hygiene was a contributory factor.[6]

Hygiene audits of hospitals began to be carried out on a national basis in 2005 and the results published.

Leas Cross

The care of older people in nursing homes and the quality of the inspection and regulation system became controversial topics in 2005 following the broadcast of a television programme exposing conditions at the Leas Cross Nursing Home in Dublin.[7] The home closed shortly afterwards in 2005.

A report by Professor Desmond O'Neill, consultant geriatrician, published in 2006,[8] described the level of care provided at the home as amounting to 'institutional abuse'. It found that persons transferred from St Ita's Hospital, Portrane, a psychiatric hospital, to Leas Cross had a median period to death of 77 days.

He noted that, according to the records he saw, 'an alarming number' of residents were in Buxton chairs.

For a maximum number of 111 residents, medical cover was provided by one doctor at a time.

He was critical of the failure by the health authorities to respond effectively to concerns raised by inspection teams and by doctors at St Ita's.

Symphysiotomy

The new century saw the emergence of a controversial issue concerning the practice of symphysiotomy in maternity hospitals in Ireland between the 1950s and the 1980s. The procedure involves sawing through the pubic bone either before or after the birth of the child when labour is obstructed. The aim is to widen the pelvis on a permanent basis.

According to a group called Survivors of Symphysiotomy, established with the help of the Women's Council of Ireland, many of the women who had this operation were left with acute pain, incontinence and other problems including impaired mobility. It was alleged that in many cases the procedure was carried out without the consent of the women themselves.

HOW THE HEALTH OF THE POPULATION HAS CHANGED (CHAPTER 10)

Most of the 19th century was characterised by outbreaks of infectious diseases which, in the words of Curry (2003), 'wrought havoc' on the population. As many as 25,000 people died in a cholera outbreak in 1832–33 alone.

The Public Health Act, 1878, aimed to prevent the spread of disease by ensuring that there was proper sanitation, that water was clean and that food was safe. Public health measures of this kind and improvements in living conditions all brought about major improvements in the health of the people.

Tuberculosis posed a major threat to health in the first half of the 20th century. In 1927, TB was killing 145 people per 100,000 of the population. By 1957, the death-rate had fallen to 24 in 100,000. Vaccinations against tuberculosis had been introduced in 1949.

Immunisation programmes greatly reduced the impact of pneumonia, whooping cough, measles, gastroenteritis and diphtheria which were leading causes of death among young children.

All the main measures of the health of the population have shown major improvements in the half century to 2007.

When the first life table was compiled in 1926, males had a life expectancy at birth of 57.4 years and females of 57.9 years. By 2002, a male baby could expect to live for 75.1 years and a female baby for 80.3 years.

Infant mortality was reduced from 68 per 1,000 live births in 1947 to 5.8 per 1,000 in 2001.

Death-rates have improved significantly. In 1960, the death-rate was 11.5% per 1,000 of the population. In 2004, it was 7%.

Cancer caused about 11% of deaths in 1950 and 25% in 2001. Heart disease continues to be the main cause of death.

In 1960, the birth-rate was 21.5% per thousand of the population. This fell to a low of 13.5% in 1995. It then began to rise again and stood at 15.3% in 2004.

The Health Education Bureau was established in 1975 and was responsible for organising programmes of health education. Non-governmental organisations such as the Irish Cancer Society and the Irish Heart Foundation did invaluable work in promoting healthier lifestyles.

In 1988, the Health Promotion Unit of the Department of Health replaced the Health Education Bureau. The 1990s saw the appointment of health promotion officers in most health boards and also the appointment of directors of public health.

The national health strategies published in 1994, *Shaping a Healthier Future*, and in 2001, *Quality and Fairness, A Health System for You*, emphasised the importance of better health and better quality of life, and not just the treating of sickness, as objects of health policy.

Surveillance of trends in infectious disease is a key public health function. The National Disease Surveillance Centre was established for this purpose in 1998. It became part of the Health Service Executive as the Health Protection Surveillance Centre when the HSE was set up in 2005.

A ban on smoking in the workplace was introduced in Ireland in 2004. At the time of the introduction of the ban, an estimated 7,000 people were dying from smoking-related diseases every year.

As a public health problem, excessive consumption of alcohol has been a feature of Irish society for well over a century. Ferriter noted that in 1891–92 there were what he called an 'astounding' 100,528 arrests for drunkenness. Publicans flourished in this atmosphere. Tralee in Co. Kerry had 117 pubs for a population of 9,367 people.

In 1961, St John of God opened a special unit for alcoholics in Dublin.

Consumption of alcohol increased dramatically at the beginning of the 21st century. *The Interim Report of the Strategic Task Force on Alcohol* (2002) reported that between 1989 and 1999, alcohol consumption per capita in Ireland increased by 41%.

Drug abuse has been a public health concern since the early 1970s. Estimates of the number of heroin addicts range from 6,000 to 13,000. Other drugs which began to be abused increasingly from the 1970s onwards included cannabis, MDMA ('ecstasy') and cocaine.

A new threat to the health of the population came in the 1980s with the development of HIV and AIDS. Between 1982 and the end

of 1999, there was a total of 691 reported cases of AIDS and 349
reported deaths.

In an effort to reduce mortality from breast cancer, the
BreastCheck programme began from February 2000 to offer free
breast screening to women aged 50–64, initially in the Eastern
Regional Health Authority, North Eastern and Midland Health
Board areas.

Vhi HEALTHCARE (PART 2)
Establishment of the VHI

Private health insurance existed in Ireland prior to the establishment of the VHI. However, it never caught the imagination of the
public in the same way that the VHI was to do and its predecessors
in the marketplace met with little success in this regard.

Under the 1953 Health Act, the 15% of the population in the
highest income group had no entitlement to free public hospital
services.

In these circumstances, the Minister for Health, T.F. O'Higgins
TD, set up an advisory body in 1955 to examine the feasibility of a
voluntary private health insurance scheme.

In its report, published in 1956, the advisory body concluded
that it was feasible to introduce 'a scheme of voluntary insurance
against the cost of hospital maintenance, of surgical and medical
services in hospital and of maternity.'

It suggested that the best type of organisation to administer
such a scheme was a non-profit-making company.

In agreeing to the establishment of the VHI, the government
rejected one of the recommendations of the advisory body: there
should be no benefit for maternity costs, it decided, on the
grounds that maternity was not an illness and therefore could be
budgeted for.

The Voluntary Health Insurance Board was appointed on 12
February 1957, under the Voluntary Health Insurance Act, 1957.

The VHI was granted a near monopoly by the Act. Only those health insurance schemes which were provided by a trade union or by a society registered in the State before the passing of the 1957 Act under the Friendly Societies Acts were allowed to continue.

Early success

The VHI was a success from the start. Membership grew steadily, from 23,238 in 1958 to 321,777 in 1968 and 645,165 in 1978. The pace of growth slowed in the 1980s but nevertheless membership exceeded one million for the first time in 1983. By the end of its first 50 years, membership stood at 1.5 million.

Pivotal to the success of the VHI then, as now, were the group schemes adopted by companies and other organisations.

The State 'played a part in promoting voluntary health insurance by offering income tax concessions and subsidies towards the cost of private accommodation but the major credit must go to the Board and its highly efficient supporting staff,' the Minister for Health and Social Welfare, Charles Haughey TD, said when opening a new public office for the VHI in 1979. The context for the relationship between the State and the VHI, as outlined by Mr Haughey, was that the VHI 'is charged with providing health insurance for those who require it on a non-profit-making basis while at the same time ensuring that the Board's operation are at all times solvent.' When the VHI was established, 'there was no guarantee of success' and 'there was then little experience in this country of carrying on health insurance on a widespread scale.'

International links

The VHI took the initiative in the establishment of the International Federation of Voluntary Health Service Funds, now the International Federation of Health Plans. The Federation was officially inaugurated in Sydney, Australia in 1968.

The first Irishman to become president of the Federation (1992 to 1994) was VHI chief executive Tom Ryan.

The 1970s and rising costs

Rising costs became a continuing concern in the 1970s. Inflation was rampant and in 1975 alone, the Consumer Price Index rose by 20.9%.

The government introduced sharp increases in charges for private beds in public hospitals in the early 1970s. The cost of claims and of administration exceeded subscription income during 1973 and 1974.

In 1979 VHI decided to guarantee that hospital and nursing home charges would be fully covered, provided a patient occupied the type of accommodation for which insurance had been arranged. The provision of full indemnity for hospital charges had been prompted by the widening of general entitlements to public hospital services.

The move was popular: during 1979–1980 the VHI enjoyed an increase of almost 21% in membership to a total of 843,309 persons.

Developments in private healthcare

In the 1970s and early 1980s, a number of important developments were in train in relation to the provision of private hospital care, an area which had seen little development for many years.

In 1974, the Religious Sisters of Charity had established St Vincent's Private Hospital beside St Vincent's University Hospital. In the following year, Mount Carmel Hospital in Dublin installed a sterile air theatre and joint replacement unit.

The Mater Hospital was drawing up plans to build a new private hospital at Eccles Street in Dublin. Across the city, consultants were planning the establishment of Blackrock Clinic.

By the end of 1986, three new private hospitals had come on stream: the Galvia in Galway, and the Mater Private and Blackrock Clinic in Dublin.

Financial crisis

These developments, together with inflation, rising charges for public hospital beds and other factors such as claims for prescribed drugs and medicines accelerated the costs being met by the VHI. At the same time, its freedom to raise premiums was restricted by government. This combination brought the organisation to a point in the late 1980s at which strong corrective action had to be taken.

Between August 1981 and January 1984 charges for semi-private and private accommodation in public hospitals increased by 369% or roughly eleven times the rate of inflation for the same period. But when the Board sought to increase subscriptions by 15.9% from 1 March 1984, only a lesser increase of 13.5% was sanctioned.

As Mr Tom Ryan, Chief Executive from 1983 to 1994, put it, 'price increases were refused and bed costs were going up all the time.'[9]

The year to the end of February 1988 brought a deficit of £12.3 million compared to a surplus of £2.9 million the previous year. The underwriting deficit was £23.7 million.

In response, the Minister for Health, Dr Rory O'Hanlon TD, appointed Mr Noel Fox, an insolvency and reconstruction expert with a knowledge of the health sector, to the post of Recovery Manager with a seat on the Board.

The out-patient scheme to reimburse the cost of prescribed medicines was identified as a major drain on resources and was discontinued. The private hospitals agreed to an 18-month price freeze.

Substantial subscription increases were introduced, though in a way which involved a lower impact on members on the most popular plan, Plan B, and in which the main burden fell on members of Plans C, D and E.

The corrective measures worked. By the end of February 1990, the underwriting deficit had been eliminated and a small surplus of £0.7 million was recorded. In the following years, the Board began to restore the reserves.

In 1993, the Department of Health announced that it would move towards charging the VHI the 'full economic rate' for private beds in public hospitals—in other words the full cost of making public facilities, such as equipment, available to private patients in public hospitals would be recouped from these patients or their insurers. This policy has since been under gradual implementation.

A new era for private hospitals
In the new century, tax incentives to encourage the building of more private hospitals were introduced in the 2001 Finance Bill.

Vhi Healthcare commissioned a Capacity Review Study (2002) by PricewaterhouseCoopers to ensure that the benefits provided under the company's plans could be provided, taking a five-year perspective. The study concluded that the already-existing capacity would meet projected demands over the period.

In his statement in the Annual Report for 2006, the chairman, Mr Bernard Collins, described the increase in private bed capacity as 'unprecedented' and 'the single biggest challenge facing private healthcare in Ireland'.

Introduction of competition
The health insurance market was opened to competition with the passing of the Health Insurance Act, 1994.

The Act reflected the policy of the government that the system of community rating should be retained. It obliged all health insurers entering the market to apply the principles of community rating, open enrolment, lifetime cover and a minimum scale of benefits.

Community rating means that older and younger people pay the same premium for the same level of cover, not only regardless of age but also regardless of health status. This principle is underwritten by a risk equalisation scheme in which companies with a disproportionately high number of young, healthy members make a transfer of funds to companies with a disproportionately high number of older, less healthy members.

The first new entrant on the Irish market was BUPA Ireland Ltd which was established in 1996.

Competition was good for the VHI. Mr Derry Hussey, Chairman from 1997 to 2003, recalled that 'competition sharpened VHI enormously'. Customer service improved, schemes expanded and membership continued to grow.[10]

Cost/income ratio

An extremely low cost/income ratio has always been a feature of VHI operations and this is an essential part of the culture of the organisation i.e. maximise the amount of premium income that is used to pay claims on behalf of members, according to Mr Vincent Sheridan, Chief Executive Officer, Vhi Healthcare. Prior to the arrival of competition in the market Vhi Healthcare's cost/income ratio was around 6.5%. Competition increased costs on marketing, customer service etc. However, in 2005 the cost/income ratio was only 8.4%. This compared with approximately 17% for BUPA and a range of 15% to 23% for other non-life insurers in the Irish market, he said.

Technology

The organisation got its first mainframe computer in 1977. An online claims assessment system was introduced in 1979. The VHI organised the first Federation of Hospital Funds IT Seminar in 1992.

In 1993, the VHI set up computer links with all the major hospitals.

Online facilities for VHI's then 7,000 corporate group schemes were introduced in 2001. In 2001 also, Vhi Healthcare's health portal, *www.vhi.ie*, was launched to provide customised lifestyle and health information to the general public and to VHI members.

Vhi Healthcare opened its business centre in Kilkenny in 2000. The business centre—which subsequently won many awards—handled inquiries and processed claims.

In 2005, a new policy administration system went live. This took two years to design and implement at a cost of approximately €30 million. In 2006 work began on a completely new claims system which will involve investment of approximately €40 million over two to three years.

White Paper, 1999, and the Health Insurance (Amendment) Act, 2001

A White Paper published by the government in 1999 promised the introduction of risk equalisation, the incorporation of Vhi Healthcare with full commercial freedom and an investment of up to €60 million by the State.

The White Paper was followed by new legislation, the Health Insurance (Amendment) Act, 2001, which made important provisions in relation to competition, commercial freedom and community rating. These included:

1. Removal of constraints on covering GP, dental, out-patient and other 'ancillary' health services.
2. Establishment of the Health Insurance Authority with the power to recommend the implementation of risk equalisation.
3. A three-year 'holiday' from risk equalisation for new insurers.
4. Provision for a 'late entry premium' which could be charged to persons taking out health insurance for the first time after the age of 35 or after a significant lapse in cover.
5. Persons aged 65 or over to be entitled to take out health insurance cover.
6. Health insurers to be allowed to reduce premiums for persons under the age of 23 in full-time education.

Risk equalisation

Although risk equalisation was provided for by the Health Insurance Act, 1994, the legislation which opened the market to competition,[11] it was not implemented until 1 January 2006, nine years after the arrival of the first competitor into the market.

In December 2005, the Minister for Health and Children, Mary Harney TD, announced that she had decided to accept a recommendation from the Health Insurance Authority that risk equalisation be commenced. Risk equalisation would be in place from 1 January, she said.

The announcement came during a year in which Vhi Healthcare incurred a €32.3 million loss, largely because of the delays in introducing risk equalisation.

Commercial freedom and changes in corporate status

The status of Vhi Healthcare and the legislation which governed it placed limits both on the organisation's ability to diversify its products and on its freedom to implement price increases.

The 1999 White Paper promised to change this and in December 2005, the Minister for Health and Children, Ms Mary Harney TD, announced that legislation would be introduced to address the issue.

The proposed changes to the corporate structure of Vhi Healthcare would give it more commercial freedom and would also see the VHI incorporated as a semi-state body in 2012. This would oblige the organisation to achieve the level of financial solvency necessary to receive authorisation as a licensed insurer by that date (the government has since decided that this target should be achieved by the end of 2008). Reserves stood at 27.1% of premium income at the end of February 2007 compared with the 40% ratio likely to be required by the Financial Regulator prior to the granting of an insurance license.

Commercial freedom would mean, among other things, that Vhi Healthcare would no longer be required to notify the Minister for Health and Children of proposals to increase premiums and it would no longer be required to seek approval from the Department of Health and Children before it introduced new products or changed existing products.

Product and service development

The new century began with the enrolment of Vhi Healthcare's 1.5-millionth member in October 2000. The market had matured to a point at which the potential for adding extra members was quite limited. This factor, together with competition and a thriving economy, led naturally to a significant expansion in the number and types of products and services offered by Vhi Healthcare, even given the statutory limitations on its commercial freedom.

The first 50 years ends on the brink of change

By the end of its first 50 years, and following a decade of competition, Vhi Healthcare had 1.57 million members and 75% of the health insurance market. A change in corporate status, giving the organisation commercial freedom, was imminent.

Chapter 2 ∾

HOSPITALS—EXPANSION, CONTRACTION AND RESISTANCE

INTRODUCTION

Almost a decade into the 21st century, the configuration of the Irish hospital service is not greatly different to that which prevailed in the closing decades of the previous century. Controversy continues, as it has done for the best part of a century, over the issue of rationalising hospital services and in particular of changing the role of smaller hospitals. What is different is that for the first time in history there is a serious government proposal to quickly expand the number of private hospital beds. That too is controversial.

At a time when the hospitals are able to deliver a more skilful range of services than ever before, public dissatisfaction with hospital services is broadly greater than ever before. Delays in overcrowded A&E departments coupled with the cancellation of planned procedures due to a relative shortage of hospital beds have left an expanding population critical of health administrators and politicians alike.

ORIGINS

The Irish hospital system comprises three distinct types of hospitals. These are public, voluntary and private.

Many public hospitals had their origins in workhouses built in the 19th century or in infirmaries attached to workhouses. The workhouses were established by local authorities under the Poor Law system and, unlike their English counterparts, had infirmaries attached to them. Over time, their role changed and they became rudimentary institutions in Ireland for the sick, the infirm, for old persons who had nowhere else to live and for other marginalised persons. Barrington (1987) notes that almost 40 infirmaries were established under legislation passed by the Irish parliament in the 18th century.[1] In the 1920s, the workhouses were abolished and the system of county hospitals, nowadays so fiercely defended by local interests, began to develop (Curry, 2003).[2] Investment in public hospitals from the 1940s onwards has seen this sector produce centres of excellence at regional level. Examples include Cork University Hospital, University College Hospital, Galway, and the Midwestern Regional Hospital, Limerick.

The oldest hospitals in the country are the voluntary public hospitals, described in the remainder of this book by the term 'voluntary hospitals' by which they are better known. Some trace their origins back to the 18th century. They were established largely by charities and later by religious orders. The voluntary hospitals tended to be located in the bigger cities and especially in Dublin.

Voluntary hospitals have traditionally been independent of the public system in their management. However, they are almost entirely reliant on public funding and deliver the same services to the same people as do the public hospitals.

Many of the voluntary hospitals have also become centres of excellence. Among the better known are St Vincent's University Hospital, Elm Park, founded by the Religious Sisters of Charity in Dublin in 1834; the Mater Hospital, Dublin, founded by the Sisters of Mercy in 1861; the Mercy University Hospital in Cork founded by the Sisters of Mercy in 1857; and Tallaght Hospital, made up of three voluntary hospitals, the Meath, the Adelaide and the National Children's Hospital (Harcourt Street) which moved out of Dublin city centre in 1998. The official name of Tallaght Hospital is the Adelaide & Meath Hospital incorporating the National Children's Hospital.

The hospital system also includes long-stay hospitals, public, voluntary and private. Those district hospitals that have survived have, by and large, become long-stay hospitals which also provide respite and rehabilitation care. The district hospitals were staffed by nurses and served by a local GP as medical officer (Hensey, 1979).[3] While long-stay hospitals have received relatively little attention in public debate, there has been a growing acknowledgment of their importance because of the expected increase in the numbers of frail, elderly people who would otherwise have to be accommodated in acute hospital beds and because of the high cost of private nursing home care.

Specialist hospitals treating cancer, tuberculosis, other infectious diseases, and orthopaedic complaints were established, mainly as voluntary hospitals, and many continue to flourish though their roles have changed or are in the course of changing.

Historically, private hospitals have been few in number. That a percentage of beds in public and voluntary hospitals has been designated for private patients has tended to inhibit the demand for private hospitals. Most private hospitals to date have been established by religious orders. Sometimes they are on the same campus as the voluntary public hospital run by the same religious order. St Vincent's Private Hospital, for instance, is beside St Vincent's voluntary hospital and the Mater Private Hospital is beside the Mater voluntary hospital though the ownership of the Mater Private Hospital has changed hands.

The Hospitals Commission was the first of a number of bodies established to advise on the funding of the hospital system. Specifically it advised on the distribution of funds generated by the Irish Hospital Sweepstakes for the development of hospitals generally. As explained elsewhere,[4] the Irish Hospital Sweepstakes were initiated by the voluntary hospitals but so successful did 'the Sweeps' become that the first Fianna Fáil government which took office in 1932 decided that money raised by the Sweepstakes should be used for the development of hospitals generally.[5] The Hospitals Commission Report for 1933–36 suggested that hospitals be developed at twelve main centres, with county hospitals only in remote areas.[6] Provincial towns would be served by district hospitals. In Dublin, it suggested, a cluster of small hospitals should be replaced by two general hospitals on the south and two on the north side of the city (Barrington, 1987).

However, the government of the day had already embarked on a programme of building, extending and developing county hospitals with the money generated by the Irish Hospital Sweepstakes. It rejected the Hospital Commission's recommendations in favour of developing both regional and county hospitals (the latter generally had one surgeon and one physician at consultant level). The broad elements of the Hospitals Commission Report were to be echoed in the Fitzgerald Report of 1968.

THE FITZGERALD REPORT

The 1960s was a period of re-appraisal of the health services and the work done in this period led to the modernisation of the health services which commenced with the Health Act, 1970. The Fitzgerald Report[7] was produced as part of this re-appraisal process by a consultative council set up by Seán Flanagan TD, Minister for Health, in 1967. The Council was chaired by Professor Patrick Fitzgerald, professor of surgery at University College Dublin, and its role was to review the hospital system.

The Council, which was made up entirely of hospital consultants, recommended that the country be served by four regional hospitals, each with 600–1,000 beds. Two of these would be located in Dublin, one in Cork and one in Galway. The regional hospitals would be linked to twelve general hospitals, each of which would have a minimum of 300 beds. Each of these general hospitals would have about 120,000 people in its catchment area. County hospitals would, in some cases, become general hospitals and in other cases become akin to district hospitals in their role and staffing. Those county hospitals which did not become general hospitals would become 'community health centres'. They would have some in-patient beds, overseen by family doctors, and diagnostic and out-patient facilities, and would provide long-stay facilities for older people. District hospitals would continue but would not play a role in acute hospital care. Nobody would be more than 60 miles from an acute hospital, the Council calculated.

That there was a need for substantial change in the way hospitals were organised had already been signalled by a White Paper, *The Health Services and their Further Development* (1966).[8] The White Paper had made the point that more people were being treated in regional hospitals and that medical care was becoming increasingly complex. This, it said, 'must lead to a recognition that the county hospital is not entirely suited to be a self-contained unit.' The county hospitals, it suggested, should be linked with each other and with regional hospitals.

These proposals were seen by the supporters of county hospitals as a threat to their viability. As Barrington (1987) points out the downgrading, as it was called, of the county hospital would mean a loss of prestige, income and jobs to the local community. In the face of fierce opposition from supporters of county hospitals, the Minister for Health accepted the Fitzgerald Report in its general principles but not necessarily in its specific recommendations (Hensey, 1979). As happened in the case of the report of the Hospitals Commission in the 1930s, the government of the day avoided a major clash with local interest groups. However, Comhairle na nOspidéal, appointed in 1972, was able to bring some degree of rationalisation to hospital services through its regulation of the appointment of specialist consultants from 1972.

THE GENERAL HOSPITAL DEVELOPMENT PLAN, 1975

A new attempt to reorganise hospitals was made in the *General Hospital Development Plan of 1975*, published by the then Minister for Health, Brendan Corish TD. It was based on consultation with health professionals, administrators and with Comhairle na nOspidéal.

It was, as Curry (2003) suggests, a document which sought to accommodate both political and health considerations.[9] It suggested twice as many general hospitals (23) as Fitzgerald (12). Nobody should be more than 30 miles away from a general hospital, it suggested, and this, again, was half the distance suggested by Fitzgerald. It was vague on some other details, such as hospital development in the cities of Cork and Limerick.

The Coalition government which published the *General Hospital Development Plan* was replaced by a Fianna Fáil government in 1977. Fianna Fáil, in its manifesto, had promised to preserve the role of the county hospitals. However, the 1980s was to usher in more than a decade of spending restrictions and cutbacks which would 'rationalise' hospital services in a more crude way than anybody had envisaged.

THE CUTBACKS OF THE 1980s AND EARLY 1990s

The cutbacks of the 1980s and early 1990s were motivated, not by a desire to develop hospital services in a particular way, but by the imperative of reducing the level of indebtedness into which the country had fallen. They affected the full range of public services but certainly the most noticeable effect was on the health services.

The cutbacks saw the closure of a number of the smaller public voluntary hospitals. Thousands of hospital beds were removed from the system. In 1980 there were 17,665 acute hospital beds in the country. By 2000 this had fallen to 11,832. Between 1984 and

1993 as many as 6,000 beds were closed. Curry (2003) notes that these changes came about, not as part of a coherent national plan, but through cuts in the budgets allocated to health boards and through withdrawing funding from some voluntary hospitals.[10]

Thus, the process of orderly development and rationalisation envisaged by reports from 1936 forward did not take place.

Curry (2003) notes, though, that in Dublin hospitals were eventually rationalised along the lines proposed by the 1975 *General Hospital Development Plan*. The city has six general hospitals as envisaged by the plan. These are, on the north side, Beaumont, James Connolly Memorial Hospital and the Mater and, on the south side, St James's, St Vincent's and Tallaght. Tallaght Hospital incorporates the Adelaide and Meath hospitals and the National Children's Hospital, Harcourt Street.

But change takes time in the Irish health system. The *General Hospital Development Plan* was published in 1975—Tallaght Hospital opened in 1998, more than two decades later!

THE 1990s AND GROWING DEMANDS ON HOSPITALS
As the population grew and the economy boomed in the 1990s, the demand on hospital services increased. With that increased demand came increased public frustration with waiting lists and with delays in A&E departments.

The decade began with the extension of an entitlement to free hospital service to the entire population in 1991. But, as Curry (2003) points out, the number of people on the waiting list for planned surgical and other procedures remained at an average of about 30,000 throughout the decade. Though it would later emerge that the figure was exaggerated by duplication and other factors, waiting lists were a major source of discontent from the 1990s onwards.

Also a major source of dissatisfaction were reports of major delays in A&E departments. Complaints about the necessity for patients, especially elderly people, to spend long periods on trollies while awaiting admission to a hospital ward were aired on the news media on a weekly, if not daily, basis.

It was partly in response to these complaints that the government published its *Quality and Fairness, A Health System for You* in November 2001. The health strategy promised the provision of 3,000 extra public beds by 2011. It also promised that no adult would wait more than three months for a planned procedure once they had seen a consultant.[11] Where necessary, treatment would be purchased from private hospitals in the Republic, Northern Ireland, the UK or elsewhere in order to meet this target. The National Treatment Purchase Fund[12] began to pay for treatments for public patients in 2002.

A hospitals agency would also be set up, the 2001 document stated. The agency would prepare a strategy to increase the capacity of acute hospitals to treat patients. It would also advise the Minister for Health and Children on issues relating to acute hospital services. In a move which reflected this undertaking, a National Hospitals Office was established as part of the Health Service Executive[13] in 2005. This measure had been proposed in the *Audit of Structures and Functions in the Health System* by Prospectus Management Consultants (2003).[14]

RATIONALISATION AGAIN—THE HANLY REPORT

A cull of hospitals and of hospital beds had taken place in the 1980s, not on the basis of recommendations made by committees over the decades, but because of the need to reduce the national debt.

In the new century another external force seemed set to force government to reorganise the hospital system.

This was the *European Working Time Directive* which, from August 2004, limited the working week for non-consultant hospital doctors to 58 hours. The length of the permitted working week would gradually be reduced further to 48 hours.

In order to respond to the Directive in a planned way, the then Minister for Health, Micheál Martin TD, established a task force, the National Task Force on Medical Staffing, which reported in 2003. The task force was chaired by Mr David Hanly and its report became known as the Hanly Report.[15]

The task force was given the job of working out how the *European Working Time Directive* could best be implemented in the hospital system. But recognising that this would require a reorganisation of the system, the terms of reference obliged the task force 'to devise, cost and promote the implementation of a new model of hospital service delivery.'

The task of this body, therefore, was nothing less than to work out how the hospital system might be reconfigured. Like its predecessors in the 1930s and the 1960s, the Hanly Report suggested that acute hospital services should be reorganised on a population basis. Each population of about 350,000 people would be served by a network of hospitals. At the centre of the network would be a regional hospital. The smaller hospitals, particularly the county hospitals, would no longer be acute hospitals in the normal sense but would provide out-patient clinics staffed on a rota basis by consultants from the regional hospitals. Elective surgery, mainly on a day basis, would be performed in them. These hospitals would also have convalescent beds and other services. Small injuries clinics would be run by nurses at the hospitals. Remote areas would be served by general hospitals rather than regional hospitals.

As happened in the case of the Fitzgerald Report, Hanly's recommended reorganisation was seen as a downgrading of the county hospital. A well-organised opposition to the suggestions emerged. A second group chaired by Mr Hanly to work out how the Report should be implemented was disbanded.

Some took this as the end of the Hanly reforms. This, however, may not be so. The Secretary General of the Department of Health, Mr Michael Scanlan, told the Dáil Public Accounts

Committee in October 2005 that the implementation of the Hanly reforms remained on the agenda of the health services 'whether you call it Hanly or call it what you will.'[16]

PRIVATE HOSPITALS

For most of the period covered by this book, and indeed for most of the period before that, private hospitals have played a relatively modest role in the Irish hospital system. However, as the period came to an end there were strong indications that this might be about to change.

As explained earlier, private hospitals were generally established by religious orders. Some were effectively on the same campus as the accompanying voluntary hospital. Others, such as the hospitals run by the Bon Secours sisters, were stand-alone hospitals in their own right.

Traditionally, private patients have tended to be treated in beds allocated for that purpose in public or voluntary hospitals. For the past twenty years the ratio of treatment in public versus private hospitals has been approximately 50:50 and it is now increasing towards the private hospital area.

The latter part of the period has seen the withdrawal of religious orders from some of their involvement with private hospitals. Private hospitals have been sold or closed by the religious orders, a move inspired mainly by a fall in vocations. While private hospitals today continue to be owned by religious orders, recent developments in this area have been financed by private sector investors.

For new private hospitals, it has always been crucial to their financial health that treatment in those hospitals is covered by the VHI. As effectively the only health insurer for most of the period, the VHI has therefore had to take a view on whether there was a necessity for the new beds and on the way in which the new beds would affect its own finances.

This topic is dealt with in more detail in Part Two but the VHI did not give developers an assurance that their facilities would be covered. This was on the basis that no assurance of continuing cover was ever given to existing hospitals.

The environment for the future of private hospitals improved when tax incentives were introduced in the Finance Bill, 2001, to encourage such developments.[17] In 2005, the Minister for Health, Mary Harney TD, instructed the Health Service Executive to implement a policy to encourage the private sector to invest in new co-located hospitals. Co-located hospitals are private hospitals built on the same campus as a public or voluntary hospital.[18]

Defending her policy in a speech to the Inaugural National Private Healthcare Conference in 2006, she pointed out that there were 2,500 private beds already within public and voluntary hospitals and that the State subsidised the running costs of these beds. The building of new private hospitals would free up to 1,000 beds in the public hospitals, she stated. The Minister also defended the scheme on the grounds that it would attract capital otherwise likely to flow out of the country into foreign property.[19]

This was a major development in government policy towards private hospitals. For the first time the provision of private hospitals was presented as an instrument of government health policy as well as of investment policy. The policy appeared to bring private hospitals in from the cold and to give them a major role in the health service. At the time of writing, the degree to which this will be implemented remains to be seen.

CONCLUSION

As the period ended, a new administrative structure had been put in place in the form of the Health Service Executive. The HSE was set to carry out its role in relation to hospitals through its own National Hospitals Office. The HSE began its work in an atmosphere of public cynicism and mistrust of health administrators. At the same time, government policy laid down that the private hospital sector would be developed to a greater extent than before and as the period ended, the HSE had begun to implement this policy.

Despite reports recommending the contrary from 1936 on, more than 40 acute hospitals remained in place. Acute hospitals continued, in the absence of the sort of economic imperatives which characterised the cutbacks of the 1980s, to be the untouchables of the Irish health services, at least in relation to their continued existence and status.

Chapter 3 ∽

CARE IN THE COMMUNITY —COMMUNITY CARE AND PRIMARY CARE

INTRODUCTION

The provision of community care was severely limited before the 1970s. From the mid-19th century, the dispensary system employed salaried doctors to treat the poorest in the population and to supply free prescribed medicines. But conditions were often primitive and there was a stigma attached to attending the dispensary. Some public health nursing was provided by the health authorities and some by voluntary groups.

The 1970s saw the beginnings of a community care system with public and private patients treated by the same GPs in the same premises, public health nursing provided by health boards, and the development of home help and other services by voluntary organisations and health boards.

The issue of how and where services for older people should be provided drove forward the development of community care. In particular the policy position, adopted in the 1960s, that older people should be enabled to live in their own homes for as long as possible, required major improvements in community care.

But these and other improvements came slowly as the country passed through economic difficulties and as shortcomings in hospital care grabbed the headlines.

By the end of the period, though, with the country in an era of economic boom, the Health Service Executive saw community care as the answer to overcrowding in hospitals. Overcrowding was leading to cancellation of elective procedures and lengthy waits for admission from A&E departments. Better community care could keep some people out of hospital and could enable others to leave hospital earlier.

Underpinning the proposed enhancements in community would be a major improvement in primary care with the promise of hundreds of new primary care teams by the end of the decade.[1]

ORIGINS

For more than a century, community healthcare as provided by the State was based largely on the dispensary system and on measures to reduce the incidence and spread of infectious diseases.

The dispensary system, which persisted until 1972, was introduced by the Poor Relief (Ireland) Act, 1851. Under the Act, the country was divided into dispensary districts. Each district employed a salaried doctor, known as a District Medical Officer, whose role was to provide free medical care to the poor of the area. The doctor was also entitled to offer a private practice for persons who did not qualify for dispensary services. Private patients were seen at the doctor's own home or at another location separate from the dispensary.

A major disadvantage of the dispensary system was that it made a distinction between the poor and the better off in the delivery of medical services (Curry, 2003).[2] While those who could pay were seen in their doctor's own surgery, the public patient had to apply for a 'red ticket' from an official authorised under the Poor Law system and then travel to a dispensary to see the doctor. Curry notes that the 1966 White Paper, *The Health Services and their Further Development*,[3] saw this discrimination as outweighing the advantages of the system. It also seems likely that visiting the dispensary was by no means a pleasant experience—in some instances it was designed in such a way as to discourage people from using it (Boland, 1997).[4] This same principle was applied to workhouses.

It is perhaps a comment on the status of health services for the poor that the dispensary system was allowed to continue until 1972. Dispensaries did not benefit, as Barrington (1987) points out, from Hospital Sweepstakes funds and patients continued to be treated in primitive conditions. In Dublin, as the city expanded into the new areas of Crumlin, Kimmage and Ballyfermot, the number of dispensary doctors was not increased to meet the new demand. In the 1930s, Barrington notes, it was revealed in a Dáil debate that dispensary doctors in Dublin on average were responsible for treating 6,220 patients each.[5]

The dispensary system was brought to an end by the Health Act, 1970. The Act made provision for a choice-of-doctor scheme based on the principle that there should be no discrimination against public patients in terms of service delivery. Public and private patients would see the doctor in the same surgery.

The new scheme immediately removed stigma which had been inherent in the dispensary system. In one dispensary seen by the author (in Caragh, Co. Kildare) the dispensary was located in the same building as the parish school in a cluster which included the village grocery shop, public house, church and graveyard. Thus, there was simply no question of privacy for persons attending the dispensary.

THE MEDICAL CARD SCHEME

Under the Choice of Doctor General Medical Services Scheme, which replaced the dispensary system, persons whose income was below a certain limit were entitled to free consultations with the GP of their choice and to free prescribed medicines.

The GP was paid by the State for each consultation under what was known as the 'fee-per-item' system. The amount paid varied according to whether the patient was seen in the GP's surgery or in the patient's home, whether the patient was seen during normal working hours etc. This arrangement continued until 1989 when a system of paying GPs an annual capitation fee per patient was introduced.

The fee-per-item system had come under criticism on the basis that, in itself, it led to higher costs (Curry, 2003). The Irish College of General Practitioners pointed out that:

> The GP's income depends entirely on the number of face-to-face consultations which can be fitted into each day. It medicalises minor illness and induces unhealthy doctor dependence in the patient.[6]

In effect, the scheme encouraged doctors to bring patients back excessively often; and because consultations tended to result in prescriptions being written, the cost of drugs was higher than it would otherwise have been.

Boland (1997) points out, though, that while the average number of consultations annually per patient rose under the fee-per-item system, the number of GPs also rose with the result that average earnings for each GP remained constant.

The system was by no means perfect for GPs either. There was no specific provision for pensions, sick leave, the cost of equipment or other expenses associated with running a practice.

Under the Capitation Scheme, introduced in 1989, the GP receives an annual fee per General Medical Service (GMS) patient. The annual fee varies according to the age of the patient and some other factors. The doctor's income is supplemented by additional allowances towards the cost of sick leave, pensions and other expenses.

The government also sought to control expenditure by rewarding doctors who kept prescription costs within a given target. The reward is given in funds for the purchase of equipment and other investments. This latter scheme has been described by Boland (1997) as 'amongst the most successful schemes in Europe in achieving its targets.'[7]

Persons qualify for free treatment as GMS patients by applying for, and being awarded, a medical card.

Those entitled to a medical card were defined by the 1970 Health Act as, 'adult persons unable without undue hardship to arrange general practitioner, medical and surgical services for themselves and their dependants and dependants of such persons.'

Medical cards were issued originally by the regional health boards and later (since 2005) by the Health Service Executive. Eligibility depended, in almost all cases, on a means test though there was scope for discretionary granting of medical cards by health board and, later, HSE officials.

In 1972, the proportion of the population covered by the medical card was 29%. This rose to a peak of 37.4% in the mid-1980s. It then declined steadily to 28.5% in 2004 (Mangan, 2004).[8]

This decline can be attributed partly to a booming economy and partly to a means test which no longer reflected the reality of Irish wages.

In 2001, every person over the age of 70 was given an automatic entitlement to the medical card regardless of means.

An additional form of entitlement to GP care—the GP Visit Card—was introduced in 2005. The card entitles persons whose means exceed the guidelines for the medical card to see their GP free of charge.

However, unlike the medical card, the Visit Card does not cover the cost of prescribed medicines. Persons holding GP Visit Cards can avail of the Drugs Payments Scheme under which no individual or family need pay more than (in 2006) €85 per month for approved prescribed medicines (see overleaf).

PRIMARY CARE—A NEW DIRECTION

The *Health Strategy, 2001* outlined a vision of primary care in which the provision of services in the community would become the core of the health service generally. This section of the strategy was published separately under the title *Primary Care: A New Direction*. The strategy is unequivocal in its statement of the importance of primary care and, by extension, community care:

> The 2001 health strategy sets out a new direction for primary care as the central focus of the delivery of health and personal social services in Ireland. It promotes a team-based approach to service provision which will help to build capacity in primary care and contribute to sustainable health and social development.[9]
>
> The aims of the proposed developments are:
> ... to provide
> (a) a strengthened primary care system which will play a more central role as the first and ongoing point of contact for people with the healthcare system,
> (b) an integrated, inter-disciplinary, high-quality, team-based and user-friendly set of services for the public, and
> (c) enhanced capacity for primary care in the areas of disease prevention, rehabilitation and personal social services to complement the existing diagnosis and treatment focus.

'Primary care,' it said, 'needs to become the central focus of the health system.'

The strategy made it clear that primary care involves a broad range of services provided by an equally broad range of professionals:

The term 'primary care' is often used synonymously with 'general practice'. While general practice is a key element, it is broader than general practice alone. It encompasses a wide range of health and personal social services delivered by a variety of professions.

It summarised as follows the way in which the new system would work:

> The health strategy proposes the introduction of an inter-disciplinary team-based approach to primary care provision. Members of the primary care team will include GPs, nurses/midwives, healthcare assistants, home helps, physiotherapists, occupational therapists, social workers and administrative personnel. A wider primary care network of other primary care professionals such as speech and language therapists, community pharmacists, dieticians, community welfare officers, dentists, chiropodists and psychologists will also provide services for the enrolled population of each primary care team.
>
> The population to be served by a team will be determined by encouraging GPs to join together their existing lists of enrolled individuals and families, within certain geographic consid-erations. This geographic focus will strengthen the capacity of the primary care team to adopt population health approaches to service provision.

In the years immediately following the publication of the strategy, progress was very slow. However, the plan received a boost when the HSE stated, in the autumn of 2006, that it would establish 500 primary care teams across the country in the next four years.[10]

PRESCRIBED MEDICINES
Patients who attended dispensaries, up to 1972, were usually supplied with medicines by the dispensary doctors themselves. In

some cases a pharmacist attended the dispensary to issue medicines.

This arrangement ended when the dispensaries were closed and the Choice of Doctor Scheme introduced. Under the new arrangement, patients received their prescribed medicines free of charge from retail pharmacists.

The Health Act, 1970, also provided for free prescribed drugs for persons with certain long-term ailments. This eventually became the Long-Term Illness Scheme. Sixteen conditions are covered by the scheme.

A scheme to enable people who did not qualify for medical cards to recoup part of the cost of prescribed drugs was introduced in 1971. The scheme was refined over the years. By the end of the period it was known as the Drugs Payments Scheme, having replaced the Drugs Refund Scheme and the Drugs Cost Subsidisation Scheme in 1999. Under the Drugs Payments Scheme, no individual or family has to pay more than €85 per month for approved prescribed medicines.

A scheme to enable VHI members to recoup the cost of prescribed drugs and medicines was introduced in 1967 and proved immediately popular. However, it also proved very costly and was discontinued when the organisation cut costs to deal with losses in the late 1980s.[11]

OLDER PEOPLE

The issue of community care has assumed particular importance in relation to older people. From the 1970s onwards, the provision of services to older people outside institutions—to enable them to remain in their own homes—has increasingly been seen as a core aim of health policy. However, it cannot be said that this aim has been pursued with the vigour that might be expected.

Prior to the 1970s, older people unable to care for themselves, and who did not have a family able or willing to care for them, were accommodated in County Homes. These County Homes, in many cases, had previously been workhouses and conditions tended to be poor.

As Coakley (1997) points out, the 130 workhouses which were opened in Ireland in the 19th century eventually became institutions for people who were old and infirm.

The first government of the Irish Free State set about the creation of a new system. All but 33 of the workhouses were closed down. The 33 which remained became County Homes, again mainly intended for people who were old and infirm. However, they also became places in which other marginalised people, including unmarried mothers and people with mental handicaps, were institutionalised.

Conditions were extremely poor with no running water supply and in many cases no sanitary provisions and no baths (Coakley, 1997).[12]

This state of affairs continued until 1968 when the *Care of the Aged* report was published.[13]

This report marks the beginning of a more modern attitude towards the needs of older people. *Care of the Aged* pointed to the unsuitability of County Homes and suggested they be replaced by new institutions to be known as Welfare Homes.

Crucially, the report advocated that as a matter of policy older people should be enabled to live in their own homes for as long as possible.

The implementation of this recommendation would require the development of community care services. These services would include chiropody, social work, occupational therapy, and medical and nursing care provided while older people were still living at home. Day hospitals should be developed and geriatric assessment units should be set up in general hospitals. Older people admitted to these hospitals should be discharged home or to other suitable accommodation as soon as possible. The County Homes, as mentioned above, should be replaced by Welfare Homes with suitable facilities and a more pleasant environment.

A National Council for the Aged should be set up to promote the welfare of older people.

The report strongly influenced government policy (Coakley, 1997). The value of both the contributory and the non-contributory old-age pensions was increased in real terms. Extra benefits such as free telephone rental and free travel were introduced.

Approximately 30 Welfare Homes were built as was sheltered housing.

Financial schemes to enable older people to live at home, such as grants for house repairs, were introduced.

The appointment of consultants in geriatric medicine to hospital geriatric departments was recommended by Comhairle na nOspidéal in 1975.

Many of the community services for older people were developed by voluntary organisations as well as by public authorities. In 1971, the Minister for Health, Erskine Childers TD, acknowledged this by appointing the National Social Service Council (later Comhairle, now the Citizens Information Board) to encourage the coordination of these services and to provide training.

These services included a home help service, developed by the health boards, meals on wheels and day care.

Despite the change of direction signalled by *Care of the Aged*, a subsequent report, *The Years Ahead: Policy for the Elderly* (1988), found that the situation remained unsatisfactory. The County Homes, it declared,

> have become geriatric hospitals, [but] too much of the atmosphere of the older institution survives in some centres.[14]

The report suggested the development of rehabilitation and day-care services to enable people to live in their own communities for longer.

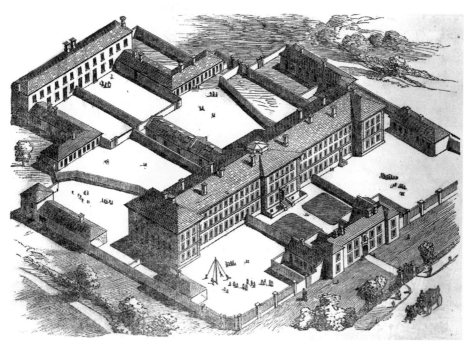

(*Hulton Archive/Getty Images*)

The Irish public hospital system has its roots in the infirmaries attached to workhouses built in the nineteenth century.

(*Topfoto*)

Florence Nightingale was a major influence on the development of nursing as a profession in Ireland. (*Topfoto*)

Medical team circa 1890. A group of doctors and nurses pose for a photograph outside their hospital. (*Hulton Archive/Getty Images*)

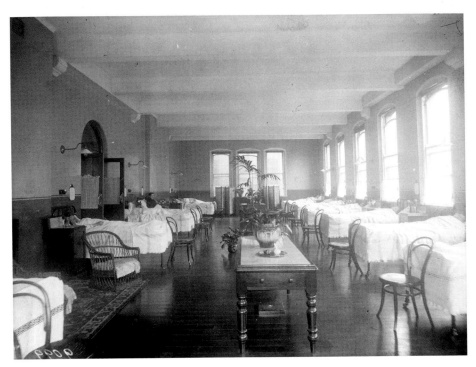

A ward in the Rotunda Maternity Hospital, Dublin, November 1912. The first maternity training hospital in Ireland, it dates from 1745 and remains one of the three major maternity facilities in the capital. (*Hulton Archive/Getty Images*)

Many workhouses evolved into county homes which later became geriatric hospitals. This is an early photograph of Newcastle Hospital, Co. Wicklow. (*Courtesy of the National Library of Ireland*)

The old Ministry of Pensions Hospital in Blackrock, Co. Dublin, later became a geriatric facility. (*Courtesy of the National Library of Ireland*)

The Hospitals Trust Fund raised money internationally from sweepstakes on horse racing and was a key contributor to the development of hospitals for almost fifty years. (*Hulton Archive/Getty Images*)

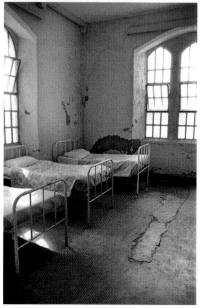

Our Lady's Psychiatric Hospital, Cork. Psychiatric hospitals were the mainstay of mental health services for many decades, but conditions were poor and many inmates had nowhere else to go. (*Derek Speirs*)

Queen Victoria donated money collected for her Golden Jubilee in 1887 to provide district nurses for rural areas. (*Hulton Archive/Getty Images*)

In 1946, Seán MacEntee TD (*front right*), as Minister for Local Government and Public Health, proposed a free GP service for 75 per cent of the population, but was opposed by the Irish Medical Association. (*Time & Life Pictures/Getty Images*)

Dr Noël Browne TD, who resigned as Minister for Health in 1951 following conflict with the Irish Medical Association and the Catholic bishops over the Mother and Child scheme. (*Lensmen Press*)

an
mátair
is
a
leanb

MOTHER
and
CHILD

WHAT THE NEW SERVICE MEANS TO EVERY FAMILY

A Department of Health brochure advertises the Mother and Child scheme. (*Father F.M. Browne S.J. Collection/The Irish Picture Library*)

T.F. O'Higgins TD. A distinguished politician and lawyer, he was Chief Justice and a Judge of the European Court of Justice. While Minister for Health in 1955, he set up the advisory body whose report led to the establishment of the VHI. (*Topfoto*)

The County Hospital, Kilkenny, is typical of hospital design in mid-twentieth-century Ireland. (*Courtesy of the National Library of Ireland*)

Tuberculosis was probably the most feared disease in Ireland in the first half of the twentieth century. This photograph shows the women's veranda of Crooksling Hospital, Blessington Road, Dublin, in 1949. (*Father F.M. Browne S.J. Collection/The Irish Picture Library*)

Seán Flanagan TD, Minister for Health, set up a consultative council in 1967 which produced the Fitzgerald Report on rationalising the hospital system.

Frank Cluskey TD, Parliamentary Secretary to the Minister for Health and Social Welfare, introduced the Supplementary Welfare Allowance in 1977 to reform a system of relief payments which had its roots in Elizabethan times. (*Derek Speirs*)

Brendan Corish TD, Minister for Health, published the General Hospital Development Plan in 1975 when local opposition blocked the implementation of the Fitzgerald Report. (*Derek Speirs*)

Dr Dermot Walsh, Inspector of Mental Hospitals from 1987 to 2003, and a strong critic of poor conditions for patients. (*Derek Speirs*)

As Curry (2003) asserts, the key to the improved provision of services for older people is coordination and this is recognised in *The Years Ahead*. The report suggested that district liaison nurses be appointed to facilitate coordination.

Again, according to Coakley (1997), this report had a 'considerable influence' on the provision of services for older people. Special care teams and coordinators of services, for example, were appointed to community care districts and more community hospitals were developed. However, Coakley points out that these developments have been patchy, and transport and other deficits have made community facilities difficult for many older people to use.

Moreover, when the National Council on Ageing and Older People reviewed progress ten years after the publication of *The Years Ahead*,[15] it found little had been done to implement its recommendations in relation to community care.[16]

Perhaps one of the more visible outcomes of the absence of a comprehensive community care system for older people can be seen in the development of lobbying groups for carers. The most prominent of these is the Carers Association, founded in Dublin in 1987 following a meeting organised by Ms Iris Charles of the Dublin Council for the Aged and Mr Frank Goodwin of Dublin Corporation.

As the Association states on its website:

At that time the word 'carer' was unknown in the context of family members caring at home, and the primary objective of the Association was to place the contribution of family carers on the political agenda. Since then the Carers Association has expanded from its initial advocacy and lobbying role to include service provision.

While the government has begun to initiate some services for carers, we believe that the vast majority of Ireland's family carers still remain without vital services. These services, such as in-home respite, are essential to family carers. They allow us to continue in our roles as family carers, thus implementing government policy to care for people in their own homes for as long as possible.

Today, the Carers Association has sixteen Resource Centres and two Service Projects from which it delivers our range of services.[17]

The Association has continually drawn attention to the enormous strain on persons caring for older and infirm people in their own homes, particularly for people suffering dementia including Alzheimer's Disease.

A Carer's Allowance was introduced in 1990. Nevertheless, carers continue to complain that there are too few support services for those who keep their aged relatives at home, even though by doing so they are saving the taxpayer considerable amounts of money which would otherwise have to be paid for institutional care.

The Alzheimer Society of Ireland, founded in 1982, lobbies on behalf of persons with Alzheimer's Disease and their carers and provides services throughout the country.

In *Quality and Fairness, A Health System for You* (2001) the government acknowledged the need for more community-based services for older people. It recommended that services be brought to an adequate level over a 10-year period through a number of measures including additional day centre places.

COMMUNITY PROTECTION

The Community Protection Programme refers in particular to measures to protect the public against infectious diseases.

This role was originally assigned to the Local Government Board and later to the Department of Local Government and Public Health.

By 1940, Barrington notes, public health measures implemented by County Medical Officers had brought about a fall in the incidence of most infectious diseases.[18]

In 1947, public health functions were divided between two new departments, the Department of Health and the Department of Local Government. Measures with a mainly engineering requirement remained with the Department of Local Government. Measures which were more medical in nature were assigned to the Department of Health.

The control of infectious diseases is one of the success stories of the social services. A variety of factors combined to bring about this success. Hensey (1979) summarises the more important factors as follows:

• The development of vaccines and other prophylactic agents
• improved sanitation and hygiene
• new and better drugs
• greater public awareness of the need for prevention.

Among the successes was the elimination of tuberculosis as a major health issue, referred to elsewhere in this book.

Immunisation programmes have also reduced diseases such as smallpox, diphtheria, polio and German measles (rubella) to the point where they are no longer a source of fear or of significant levels of ill health.

The enforcement of food hygiene under the Food Hygiene Regulations, 1950, and subsequent regulations has also been a key part of the community protection programme.

The quality of foods and of drugs has been regulated under the Sale of Food and Drugs Act, 1875, and subsequent legislation.

The sale of poisons and dangerous drugs has been controlled since 1851 when, Hensey (1972) notes, controls were introduced on the sale of arsenic.[19]

The National Drugs Advisory Board (now the Irish Medicines Board) was established in 1966 to monitor new drugs and to assess the safety of drugs generally. Its successor, the Irish Medicines Board, was established under the Irish Medicines Board Act, 1995.

The IMB describes its role in this area as to:

> ensure in so far as possible, consistent with current medical and scientific knowledge, the quality, safety and efficacy of medicines available in Ireland and to participate in systems designed to do that throughout the European Union. Before a medicinal product can be authorised for use, an application must be made to the Irish Medicines Board and this must contain all of the necessary data supporting its quality, safety and efficacy.

Following approval, the IMB 'monitors the type and frequency of any reported side-effects.'

The Irish Medicines Board also monitors the quality of medicines by conducting inspections at sites of manufacture and distribution of medicines and by random sampling of products both pre- and post-authorisation. The use of medicines for clinical research purposes also falls within the IMB's remit.

In the case of veterinary medicines there must likewise be assurance of quality, safety and efficacy but in addition the consequences to human health of the use of medicines in animals must be considered.[20]

PUBLIC HEALTH NURSING

Public health nursing was originally developed on a voluntary basis and for many decades the most prominent organisation providing the service was the Queen's Institute of District Nursing in Ireland.

Money collected for the golden jubilee of Queen Victoria in 1897 had been used, on her instructions, for the selection, training and management of nurses to work in the homes of the poor. The nurses became known as the Queen's Nurses or Jubilee Nurses (O'Morain, 2004). Another scheme, the Lady Dudley Scheme, began in 1903. These were the forerunners of today's Public Health Nurses.[21]

The development of a public health nursing service by the State began in the 1950s under powers given to local authorities by the Health Act, 1947.

The role of the public health nurse was outlined by the Department of Health in 1966 in a circular which stated that:

> The object should be to provide such domiciliary midwifery services as may be necessary, general domiciliary nursing, particularly for the aged, and, at least equally important, to attend to the public healthcare of children, from infancy to the end of the school-going period. The nurses should provide health education in the home and assist local medical practitioners in the care of patients who need nursing care but who do not require treatment in an institution—whether for medical or social reasons. The aim should be to integrate the district nursing service with the general practitioner, hospital in-patient and out-patient services, so that the nurse will be able to fulfil the important function of an essential member of the community health team, and carry out her duties in association with hospital staffs and other doctors in her district.[22]

DENTAL, AURAL, OPHTHALMIC SERVICES

Dental services are provided to children under the 1970 Health Act by dentists employed full-time by the Health Service Executive.

The Health (Fluoridation of Water Supplies) Act, 1960, obliged health boards to arrange to fluoridate piped, public water supplies.

An ophthalmology service and the provision of hearing tests and hearing aids are also part of the community care programme.

CASH PAYMENTS

Part of the work of the health administration services has been the payment of certain cash benefits. These include certain allowances related to disability and illness, and also the Supplementary Welfare Allowance, a payment for persons without an income who do not qualify for a social welfare payment or are waiting for such a payment to be processed. In some cases the Supplementary Welfare Allowance supplements the social welfare payment.

The Supplementary Welfare Allowance dates back to the reign (1558–1603) of Queen Elizabeth I when Relieving Officers were appointed to give assistance to the poor in their parishes. Under the Poor Law System, introduced in the 19th century, the assistance was known as Outdoor Relief as it was provided outside the confines of a workhouse. The payment later became known as Home Assistance. It was replaced in 1977 by the Supplementary Welfare Allowance and the former Home Assistance Officers became Community Welfare Officers. On the initiative of Mr Frank Cluskey TD, then Parliamentary Secretary (Junior Minister) to the Minister for Health and Social Welfare, the new scheme reformed the Home Assistance Scheme by introducing a standardised means test.

It is interesting to note that in the early years of the 21st century, the officials administering the scheme were still known in many areas as 'relieving officers', the term introduced 500 years earlier.

CONCLUSION

Until the 1970s, the community care system was virtually non-existent by today's standards. In the decades since, the importance of community care has been increasingly acknowledged but progress in developing the system has been slow.

However, as the period ended the status of community care had risen. In particular, the 2001 health strategy had put primary care—perhaps the most critical part of the community care system—at the heart of health policy.

Following a slow start, the Health Service Executive seemed determined, by the end of the period, to push forward vigorously the development of primary care teams. Such a measure, if implemented, would mark the greatest boost for the community care concept since its endorsement at official level in the 1960s.

Chapter 4 ⌒

MENTAL HEALTH CARE— FROM THE INSTITUTION TO THE COMMUNITY

INTRODUCTION

Mental health has long been the Cinderella of the Irish health service as a whole. While funding of the general health services has been rising rapidly, some say alarmingly, mental health's share of that funding has fallen steadily over the years. Reports on how to improve the services have been produced from 1966 onwards but implementation has been slow.

The development of services in the community has been uneven and patchy throughout the country. The Inspector of Mental Hospitals, Dr Dermot Walsh, who occupied that role from 1987 to 2003, relentlessly pointed to appalling conditions in some of the older psychiatric institutions. Though his reports generated controversy, the political system was slow to respond to them.

His successor, Dr Teresa Carey, in her first report as Inspector of Mental Health Services for 2004 found poor management of mental health services; misuse of resources; uneven provision of community care; a failure to involve patients in service planning and delivery; and a host of other deficiencies.

In 2006, a new strategy document, *A Vision for Change*, was published by the government. It envisaged the closure of all psychiatric hospitals, the development of community services, greater use of 'talk therapies' such as counselling and an emphasis on recovery rather than illness.

ORIGINS

On New Year's Eve, 1958, a total of 21,046 patients were in district mental hospitals according to official returns. In other words, approximately 0.5% of the population was in a mental hospital (Walsh, 1997).[1]

In that same year St Columba's Hospital in Sligo had almost 800 patients. This represented 0.7% of the population in its Sligo/Leitrim catchment area.

In the 19th century, persons who were mentally ill may have formed the biggest single group of people being 'cared for' by the health services. Institutions were established throughout the country but, Hensey (1979)[2] points out, these institutions were lunatic asylums which did not provide nursing or adequate treatment. The Victorians had commenced the policy of transferring what were described as lunatics from workhouses, bridewells (houses of correction) and prisons to district lunatic asylums.

Many of these district asylums later became mental hospitals, usually with their own farms and often with staff and patients living on the same site. Essentially, the public and official attitude towards mental illness in the 1930s and 1940s was to confine the problem behind high walls and hide it rather than treat it (Ferriter, 2004).[3] Much of that attitude continued into the 1950s and 1960s.

The asylums and psychiatric hospitals had an economic importance which cannot be overlooked. In 1951, patients in the asylum accounted for almost half the population of Ballinasloe, Co. Galway (Walsh, 1997). Full-time employees accounted for about a fifth of those townspeople who were not mental patients. So while the incarceration of mental patients in big hospitals has long been condemned, it is interesting to note that these hospitals performed a major economic role in their immediate areas at a time when there was little else in the way of employment.

The 1945 Mental Treatment Act was a milestone in the provision of mental health services in Ireland. It reformed old legislation which had been replaced fifteen years earlier in Britain (Ferriter, 2004). One of the purposes of the Act, Ferriter notes, was to bring a halt to the practice of using the psychiatric system as a dumping ground for inconvenient persons. However, if the intention of the 1945 Act was to prevent inappropriate admissions to psychiatric hospitals, it was a very long time indeed before this desirable aim was achieved.

The key change brought about by the Act was the designation of categories of patients as voluntary or temporary. Prior to the implementation of the Act in 1947, patients were committed by means of warrants signed by Peace Commissioners. The 1945 Act provided for the signing of committal orders or reception orders by doctors. Under the old legislation there was no specific procedure for temporary or voluntary admission. These were introduced by the 1945 Act. Until the implementation of this measure in 1947, the law had simply assumed that patients with psychiatric illnesses would not willingly go to hospital and all admissions were involuntary.

The 1945 Act meant that patients could agree to enter a psychiatric hospital on a voluntary basis. This option seems to have been initially more popular among those who would be going to privately-run hospitals rather than to the big public hospitals. At the end of 1947, only 114 out of 17,791 patients living in district and auxiliary mental hospitals were voluntary; but of 882 patients in private charitable hospitals, 304 were voluntary (Walsh, 1997). By the late 1970s, however, three quarters of admissions to psychiatric hospitals were on a voluntary basis.

The 1945 Act also introduced a provision under which people who had been detained on an involuntary basis could be allowed out on what was called 'absent on trial'. This meant that persons were discharged on the basis that their condition had improved and that they could be brought back to hospital without being certified again if their condition worsened.

A WORLD APART

The mental hospitals, as mentioned earlier, had their own farms. Between them, they farmed almost 7,000 acres and the biggest farm, with almost 1,000 acres, was at St Ita's, Portrane, in North County Dublin. Farming was not solely done as a matter of self-sufficiency. According to Walsh (1997), it was also an outcome of the belief that work in itself was helpful in treating mental illness.

But the psychiatric hospitals were not there solely to treat mental illness—in many respects, they were a substitute for the provision of appropriate services elsewhere. For more than half of the 20th century new patients, as Walsh puts it, 'flooded' the psychiatric hospitals. These included many who did not belong in a psychiatric institution—children, old people, mentally handi-capped people and the socially marginalised in general with nowhere else to go, for instance. Old people were regularly admitted to psychiatric hospitals even though the then Inspector of Mental Hospitals, Dr Dolphin, warned in 1953 that their admission was often due not to a mental illness but to their living conditions (Ferriter, 2004).

Quite apart from the categories of inappropriate admissions mentioned above, persons who were inconvenient, defiant or who did not 'fit in' were in danger of committal to a psychiatric hospital for, in effect, life. There they became, in the words of Elizabeth Malcolm (1999), writing about the early years of the century but in words which were true for much of the century, a sort of 'living dead' removed from the wider society.[4]

Senior staff of these hospitals were paid in accordance with the number of beds they controlled and so were incentivised to welcome the flow rather than attempt to halt it. Little or nothing, therefore, was done to dissuade those people whose circumstances were so desperate that they turned to psychiatric institution for shelter.

By 1963, as many as 16% of people living in psychiatric hospitals were not mentally ill but had learning difficulties or other intellectual disabilities i.e. they were mentally handicapped and not mentally ill. While institutions had been set up by voluntary bodies, including religious orders, to provide residential care for mentally handicapped persons, these institutions were, according to Walsh, 'selective' in whom they accepted and this left many with no alternative but the psychiatric hospital (Walsh, 1997).

The population of mental hospitals also included unmarried mothers and children (Ferriter, 2004).

The administration of the psychiatric hospitals was to one side of that of hospitals in general. Each hospital was run by a resident medical superintendent who reported to the mental hospital board. It was not until the 1960s that there began to be a change in this with a move towards administrative integration. Essentially, the medical superintendent worked with little interference, it would appear, from any higher authority.

Indeed, Walsh describes the medical superintendent as 'autonomous and autocratic'. Most of the staff were known as attendants. Very gradually, attendants became psychiatric nurses. It was only in the mid-50s that a small number of general trained nurses began to work in the system.

Up to the middle 1950s and even into the 1960s, treatments were used which today would be greeted with horror, or were delivered in a way that would no longer be tolerated. In the 1950s, electric shock treatment (otherwise known as electro-convulsive therapy or ECT) was given without an anaesthetic or muscle relaxant. Though some depressed patients improved under ECT many suffered broken and dislocated bones because of the way it was administered (Walsh, 1997).

The 1950s and 1960s also saw the use of insulin therapy for first-onset schizophrenic patients. Insulin was administered to patients to put them into a coma and they were then given glucose to wake them up. Some patients went into irreversible coma and died. It appears from clinical trials performed in the 1960s that the coma had no beneficial effect whatever. The 1960s also saw the use of brain surgery which, however, failed to produce clinical improvements or else disabled the patients with side-effects.

ECT began to be administered in combination with anaesthetics and muscle relaxants in the 1960s and it became a particularly common form of treatment in the psychiatric hospitals for a time.

The late 1950s also saw the introduction of psychotropic drugs as antidepressants, tranquillisers and sedatives.

Conditions in the public psychiatric hospitals were bad with some hospital wards containing as many as 120 patients, an astonishing number. Ferriter (2004) refers to conditions in the district mental hospital in Clonmel in 1958. Each patient had a living space of seventeen square feet; some had to sleep on the floor; cooking utensils were stored in a lavatory; and three or four patients were bathed in the same water. The report which described these conditions was never circulated or published.

Something had to be done. Not only were conditions poor but Ireland had more psychiatric in-patients than any other country in the world—a fact which the World Health Organisation commented on in the early 1960s (Ferriter, 2004).

COMMISSION OF INQUIRY ON MENTAL ILLNESS 1961–66

What was done was to establish a Commission of Inquiry on Mental Illness in 1961. The Commission's report,[5] published in 1966, found that alternatives to hospitalisation for psychiatric patients barely existed. It went on to make a set of recommendations which today seem surprisingly modern.

The big psychiatric hospitals should gradually be replaced with psychiatric units attached to general hospitals; care should be provided in the community where possible, and by multidisciplinary teams; general practitioners should be more involved in the care of people with mental health conditions; and psychiatric services for children should be developed, it recommended.

The Commission suggested that social factors such as high unemployment, rural isolation and low marriage rates contributed to the very high reliance on psychiatric hospitals. It also noted though that the attitude of the public was unfavourable towards the discharge of patients from psychiatric hospitals.

The report of the Commission was forward-looking but it had a major flaw: as Walsh points out, it did not say how its recommendations should be implemented. This omission meant that no formal plan was ever drawn up to implement the 1966 report. Some advances took place but outside the framework of a national plan. Ardkeen Hospital in Waterford opened the first psychiatric unit in a general hospital in 1965. Some out-patient clinics were developed. Sanatoria, no longer needed now that the scourge of TB had been tamed, were, in a number of cases, turned over to the psychiatric services.

In Dublin, the Eastern Health Board established mental health services on a geographical basis with each local service headed by a clinical director.

In 1979, there were twelve private psychiatric hospitals. Cooperation between the private hospitals and health boards was growing. Between them, the private hospitals had about 1,000 places with the greatest number being in St Patrick's in Dublin with 398 in-patients at the end of 1977 (Hensey, 1979).

All in all, though, it may be said that the report of the 1966 Commission ran into the sand. In an illustration of how little had changed in the wake of the Commission's report, Curry (2003) notes that a 1981 census of psychiatric patients by the Medico-

Social Research Board found that one fifth of them had lived in hospitals for a quarter of a century or more; 80% were unmarried and about a third were over 65 years old.[6]

By contrast to other commentators, Hensey (1979) argued that the recommendations of the Commission had largely been followed in the development of policy.

A new attempt was made to develop the mental health services in a substantial way in 1981 when the Minister for Health, Eileen Desmond TD, established a study group which three years later produced the report, *Planning for the Future*.

PLANNING FOR THE FUTURE, 1984

Planning for the Future is, without doubt, the major strategic document in the history of the Irish psychiatric services to date. It envisaged that services would be provided on a localised basis; as far as was possible, people with psychiatric illnesses would be treated in a community setting; existing long-stay patients would be rehabilitated so that they too could live in the community; a psychiatry of old age would be developed; services for alcoholics would be locally based in the community to deal with the phenomenon in which male admissions to psychiatric hospitals for problems related to alcohol constituted one third of all admissions; other drug problems would also be dealt with in the community; and children's psychiatric services would be developed and extended to the whole country.

Crucially, *Planning for the Future* outlined the details of how its recommendations could be implemented.

While progress continued to be slow, from the viewpoint of those using the mental health services and of those working in them, *Planning for the Future* did, nevertheless, reshape the way mental healthcare was delivered in Ireland.

Localised services were set up in most areas and a slow but steady process of providing psychiatric units in general hospitals was undertaken. The number of psychiatric in-patients had fallen to 5,830 by the end of 1995 compared to 16,000 in 1981 when the study group that produced *Planning for the Future* was set up.

By the late 1990s, it had become the norm for mental health patients to be seen at facilities located in the community rather than in psychiatric hospitals. The number of beds for psychiatric patients had fallen as the number of day places and residential places in the community rose.

Between 1984 and 2000, the number of day places had risen from 800 to 2,349 and the number of places in community residences from 900 to 2,934 (Curry, 2003). By 2002, eighteen general hospitals had psychiatric units.

That said, though, Curry (2003) notes that the 2001 health strategy, *Quality and Fairness, A Health System for You* acknowledged that few health boards had succeeded in completing the implementation of the change from care in institutions to community care.[7]

The role of private psychiatric hospitals now began to change. St Patrick's in Dublin and St John of God had provided what Walsh called 'high-quality in-patient accommodation and treatment for patients financially supported by the Voluntary Health Insurance organisation and other insurance schemes.'[8]

As health insurers decreased the number of annual days for which they provided in-patient cover, private hospitals looked for other sources of patients.

For instance, St John of God were contracted to provide psychiatric services for the Eastern Health Board. St Patrick's was already responsible for the community services of the psychiatric hospital at the St James's Hospital complex in Dublin.

INSPECTOR OF MENTAL HOSPITALS

A major feature of public debate on the shortcomings of the mental health services throughout the period was the concern generated by the reports of the Inspector of Mental Hospitals. The last Inspector of Mental Hospitals was Dr Dermot Walsh. His reports were hard-hitting and year after year they condemned bad conditions in psychiatric hospitals. They were frequently published quite late by the Minister for Health, leading to the suspicion that some would not have been published at all but for political and media pressure. When published, Dr Walsh's reports were the subject of substantial media comment and public concern about the conditions of psychiatric patients. Even so, the political system was slow to respond to these concerns, and the government and political parties saw the improvement of conditions in general hospitals for non-psychiatric patients as their political priorities.

THE MENTAL HEALTH ACT, 2001

A *Green Paper on Mental Health* (1992)[9] and a subsequent *White Paper on Mental Health* (1995)[10] led to the passing of the Mental Health Act, 2001, which saw the establishment of the Mental Health Commission, the creation of a new Inspectorate of Mental Health Services, and the setting up of mental health review boards to consider the case of every person involuntarily detained in a psychiatric hospital.

The Mental Health Commission described the 2001 Act as 'the most significant legislative provision in the field of mental health for over 50 years. The legislation brings Irish mental health law into conformity with the European Convention for the Protection of Human Rights and Fundamental Freedoms.'[11]

THE MENTAL HEALTH COMMISSION

The Mental Health Commission, established in 2002, is the agency mainly responsible for vindicating the rights of psychiatric patients but its role goes beyond that. The Commission describes its guiding principles as:

> . . . the promotion of quality in the delivery of mental health services, the promotion of the interests of all persons availing

of mental health services and the protection of interests of persons involuntarily admitted under the provision of the Mental Health Act, 2001.[12]

It has three key areas of activity:

- The preparation and review of codes of practice and the preparation of rules and procedures for certain treatment interventions such as ECT, bodily restraint and seclusion.
- The appointment of the Inspectorate of the Mental Health Services.
- The establishment of the independent review system of those involuntarily detained in psychiatric institutions. This involves the appointment of a panel of consultant psychiatrists, the establishment of a legal aid scheme and the appointment of mental health tribunals to review the detention of those patients involuntarily detained.

A VISION FOR CHANGE

In 2006, a new strategy for the mental health services was published. *A Vision for Change* was the work of an expert group established in 2003 by the Minister of State at the Department of Health and Children, Tim O'Malley TD.

The report of the expert group both reflected the work of previous bodies and went beyond those recommendations. The changes sought by the expert group included the following:

- The State's fifteen public psychiatric hospitals should be closed over a period of ten years and the money raised should be used to fund services in the community.
- An additional 1,800 staff should be recruited for the mental health services.
- Each region of about 300,000 people should have a 'crisis house' for patients who would otherwise be admitted to a psychiatric hospital.

- The number of in-patient beds for children and adolescents with mental health difficulties should be increased from twenty to 100.
- More use should be made of 'talk therapies' such as counselling.

Its plan, it said, would mean that spending on mental health would amount to 8.24% of the total health budget. This compared to 6.98% in 2005 and 13% in 1984.

This reduction in funding of mental health services since the 1980s, it should be noted, occurred at a time when the suicide rate was rising. In the 50 years between 1945 and 1995, the suicide rate rose from 2.38 per 100,000 to 10.69 per 100,000 (Ferriter, 2004).[13] The figures for the early years could be considerably higher as coroners had a tendency, until relatively recent times, to describe suicide as accidental death. Nevertheless, there is a consensus that a real rise in suicide has occurred in recent years.

THE INSPECTORATE OF MENTAL HEALTH SERVICES

The Inspector of Mental Health Services reports to the Mental Health Commission each year, reviewing the quality of care and treatment given to persons by the services. This function is seen by the Commission as enabling it to carry out its statutory responsibility to 'promote, encourage and foster the establishment and maintenance of high standards and good practice in the delivery of mental health services.'

The new Inspectorate commenced work in 2004. In its first year's work it found a wide range of deficiencies in the way mental health services were managed and delivered. The necessary specialist services had not been developed, the Inspectorate found; the service suffered from poor management; there was a lack of accountability; there was failure to deliver mental health services efficiently; resources were mismanaged; there was a lack of capital investment in the mental health service; and patients were not being involved in service planning and delivery.[14]

There were also glaring inconsistencies in the way mental health services were delivered around the country. For instance, ECT was prescribed for 38.7 patients per 100,000 population over the age of sixteen in the Southeast area but for a fraction of that proportion, 8.4 per 100,000, in the Southern area. Twenty-four-hour staffed community places also varied remarkably in their provision. In Clare there were 187.9 such places per 100,000 over the age of sixteen. In Wexford the rate was 13.6. In Galway it was eight.

The Inspectorate noted in its report that the level of staffing of community places tended to reflect the past existence of large institutions. Areas which had a large psychiatric institution in the past now tended to have a higher level of 24-hour staff community places.

COUNSELLING

Recent years have seen a growth in the availability and use of counselling. While counselling was unheard of in the Ireland of 1957, it had become widely accepted by the end of the period. In its directory for 2005–2007, the Irish Association for Counselling and Psychotherapy—a non-governmental accreditation body—listed approximately 1,000 accredited counsellors who had undergone specified forms of training. In addition, there were counsellors who were accredited by other bodies or who were unaccredited (there are no legal restrictions on who can work as a counsellor).

Most counselling is provided on a private, fee-paying basis.

NON-GOVERNMENTAL ORGANISATIONS

A range of services, ranging from self-help to training, are provided by non-governmental organisations. Some operate as self-help groups and others also provide information, advocacy and training services. The more prominent include Schizophrenia Ireland, Mental Health Ireland, Aware, GROW and Recovery Inc.

CENTRAL MENTAL HOSPITAL

Since 1850, the Central Mental Hospital in Dundrum, Dublin, has provided psychiatric services for persons referred by the criminal justice system. According to the Minister for Health and Children, Micheál Martin TD, in 2003, it was 'probably the oldest forensic secure hospital in Europe.'[15] In a discussion paper published in 2006, the Mental Health Commission recommended that forensic psychiatry services should be provided mainly on a regional rather than a national basis and that high secure care should be provided at a re-located Central Mental Hospital.[16]

CONCLUSION

The end of the period covered by this book has seen the publication of a progressive strategy document, *A Vision for Change*, and the establishment of the Mental Health Commission. Both developments give reason to believe that the provision of mental health services is moving in a direction which respects the rights and needs of persons with mental illnesses and of persons with other mental health difficulties.

But the mental health system has serious failings, as outlined by the Inspector of Mental Health Services in her report for 2004. It also receives little attention politically and has seen its share of funding fall steadily. Therefore it is all too likely that progress will continue to be slow and uneven into the future.

Chapter 5 ～

THE HEALTH SERVICES AND DISABILITY

INTRODUCTION

The principle which underpins policy is to enable each individual with a disability to achieve his or her full potential and maximum independence, including living within the community as independently as possible. *Quality and Fairness, A Health System for You* (2001)

The principle stated in the 2001 health strategy[1] exemplifies the sea change in attitudes towards disability over the past 50 years.

Until comparatively recently, people with disabilities were hidden in hospitals, psychiatric and otherwise. To have a disability was to be excluded from society. (The position of psychiatric patients is dealt with in Chapter Four. This chapter focuses on persons with other disabilities.)

In the late 1940s and 1950s this view began to be challenged by some parents of disabled children and some disabled persons themselves, specifically recovering TB patients. Later, especially from the 1970s onwards, it was challenged by disabled people themselves. Working from a perspective informed by the principle of equality, they can claim credit for bringing about the establishment of the Commission on the Status of People with Disabilities and ultimately, the Disability Act, 2005.

While the level of services and opportunities remained unsatisfactory at the start of the new century, and the Disability Act was criticised for its limitations, there is no doubt that persons with disabilities had improved their status to an extent unthinkable in 1957.

ORIGINS

A brief look at the history of Rehab, as it is now called, can give us an insight into changing attitudes towards disability.

The Central Committee for the Rehabilitation of the Tuberculous —now Rehab—was founded in 1949 by recovering TB patients.

Disability was seen entirely as a health issue at the time. In planning to train former TB patients for work, the Committee was going against that prevailing view. Moreover, unemployment and emigration were high for able-bodied people so the concept of creating jobs for people with disabilities received little support.

Indeed, by Rehab's own account, the new Committee was viewed with hostility by State officials. The State made unsuccessful attempts to close down the workshops on health grounds. Companies refused to employ the trainees for fear they would infect others with TB.

Nevertheless, the Committee received an impetus from the Minister for Local Government and Public Health, Noel Browne TD, who asked it to help to rehabilitate former TB patients.[2]

The Committee set up a workshop in Dublin but, despite his verbal support, Noel Browne and his successors denied it State funding until the 1960s. The Rehab Institute, as it was then renamed, responded by setting up a football pools competition in 1952 to raise money. The effort was a success and Rehab opened new facilities in Dublin, Cork and Limerick.

By 1957 there were few new cases of TB and Rehab began to accept people with other disabilities, starting with psychiatric patients from St Patrick's Hospital, Dublin. Again, by Rehab's own account, most doctors regarded the attempt to train psychiatric patients for work as foolish.

But the move was a success and Rehab quickly opened its doors to all people with disabilities.

The work of local committees set up all over the country in 1961, in a failed attempt to raise £250,000, enabled it eventually, along with funding from the European Economic Community (from 1973) to provide services throughout the country.

In this short account one can see the marginalisation of disabled people within the health services and how that only gradually changed thanks to a sustained effort by those who were prepared to challenge that marginalisation.

Intellectual disability

With the exception of psychiatric patients, persons with intellectual disabilities were more marginalised than any other disabled group half a century ago.

Even children as young as seven were admitted to adult psychiatric hospitals. As noted elsewhere, the former Inspector of Mental Hospitals, Dr Dermot Walsh, attributed this practice at least partly to a choosiness on the part of the intellectual disability organisations as to who they would accept into their residential services.[3]

Ryan (1999), the mother of an autistic boy, notes in her book *Walls of Silence* that some Resident Medical Superintendents of psychiatric hospitals in the 1940s and 1950s expressed concern at the placing of persons with intellectual disabilities (or 'mental defectives' as they were called then) in their hospitals. Their concerns were largely ignored.[4]

Ryan tells of a seven-year-old boy committed to Limerick Mental Hospital in 1946 after being rejected by a disability institution in Dublin for his 'mischievous behaviour'. The psychiatric hospital found him 'quite harmless and amenable and easily managed' but could not get more suitable institutions to take him. It is not known whether this boy spent his life in a psychiatric hospital or, indeed, whether he is in a psychiatric institution to this day.

In 1947, the Fianna Fáil government had prepared legislation to provide for institutions to care for 'mental defectives' but it fell with the government the following year. The Department of Health resumed work on legislation when Fianna Fáil returned to government but, according to Ryan, it was abandoned when T.F. O'Higgins TD was Minister in 1955, in the second inter-party government, following Fianna Fáil's defeat in 1954.

Ryan notes that government in the 1950s and onwards looked to religious orders to house and provide services for persons with intellectual disabilities. As a result, she argues, the religious orders were never brought to book for selection processes which saw many persons with intellectual disabilities spending most of their lives in psychiatric hospitals.

The 1950s also saw moves by parents to ensure that their intellectually disabled children could live at home while attending special schools. This trend began with St Michael's House, established in 1955 by a group of parents and which today has community-based centres in more than 120 different locations throughout the Dublin area. Parents throughout the country followed the example of St Michael's House.

The 1980s and the 1990s saw the implementation of a policy to move persons with intellectual disabilities out of psychiatric hospitals and into more suitable facilities.

Yet, in 2005, the National Disability Authority was still calling on the State to accelerate 'the programme of transfer of people with intellectual disabilities who are inappropriately placed in psychiatric hospitals to alternative supported homes.'[5]

AN ISSUE RECOGNISED

Curry (2003) points out that over the years many groups developed which were concerned with persons with particular types of disability.[6] For instance, persons with multiple sclerosis or cerebral palsy were represented by their own groups.

As a result, there are more than 200 disability organisations affiliated to the Disability Federation of Ireland, previously called the Union of Voluntary Organisations for the Handicapped.

The existence of so many groups contributed to the equality and rights-led disability movement which achieved so much in the 1980s and 1990s.

The primary focus of most disability groups was to lobby for better social services for those with whom they were most concerned, to provide such services themselves or a mixture of both.

Much of this work was fuelled by the fears and anger of parents and relatives who received relatively little help from the State. Protests and lobbying by disability groups were a feature of the overall disability scene in the late 1980s and early 1990s.

It was only in the 1980s that the issue of services for people with disabilities and of their status in society began to be discussed in a consistent way.

When the health boards were established under the Health Act, 1970, responsibility for disability services was given to each board's Special Hospital Care Programme.

Despite this, Colgan (1997) points out that the health boards failed to integrate services in such a way as to provide a 'clear, simple path' through the system for families or individuals looking for support, whether financial or otherwise. This, she notes, was the major frustration later expressed in submissions to the Commission on the Status of People with Disabilities.[7]

Thus, there was a good deal for people to be angry about when it came to service provision and to the difficulties they experienced in finding out about these services.[8]

Aside from this frustration, a second strand—a recognition of the rights of persons with disabilities—was feeding into the movement of the 1980s and 1990s. For instance, the 1974 *Training and Employing the Handicapped* strongly supported the concept of community workshops and in doing so gave expression to the principle that persons with disabilities were entitled to full participation in their communities and to full recognition as citizens.[9] It could be, and was, argued that workshops actually separated people with disabilities from the wider community yet they represented a major change in the earlier attitude of hiding disabled people away with no regard for their wishes or capabilities.

By the 1990s, the policy and attitudes towards the position of people with disabilities had firmly changed. The provision of residential accommodation as the primary response to disability had lost favour. The goal now was to enable persons with disabilities to live as independently as possible, preferably in their own homes in the community, and to take as complete a role in the activities of society as was possible.

Perhaps it is an indication of how long people with intellectual disabilities had been 'out of sight and out of mind' that it took until 1995 for a National Intellectual Disabilities Database to be established. The database showed, in 2000, that there were 26,760 persons registered as having intellectual disabilities.

The review group report *Towards an Independent Future*, published in 1996, emphasised the view of people with disabilities as persons who should be enabled to live as independently as possible. The report saw the provision of such services as day-care nursing and personal assistants as a means towards this end.[10]

The Disabled Person's Maintenance Allowance must rank as one of the more frustrating examples of the old view of disability as a sickness and this, too, failed to survive the new attitudes of the 1980s and 1990s. The DPMA was introduced under the Health Act, 1953, and administered by health boards until 1996. There had been considerable criticism of lengthy waiting lists for the granting of the DPMA to eligible people and of the way in which the boards administered the allowance. At the end of 1976, there were 24,862 recipients of the DPMA (Hensey, 1979).[11] Even in the absence of reliable statistics on disability at that time, it is likely that this figure represented only a fraction of the number of people with disabilities in the country.

The introduction of the DPMA was significant in that it addressed some of the financial needs of disabled people within a modern framework of income maintenance rather than crudely providing for them under the old Poor Law.

But as Colgan[12] points out, the fact that the allowance was administered by the health services may have added to the impression among disabled people that there was no hope they would ever work in the open market. Indeed many were afraid to take short-term temporary employment because if they lost the allowance it would take a very long time to get it back.

The Department of Social Welfare took over the administration of the DPMA in 1996. It was later subsumed into the Disability Allowance.

THE RIGHTS AND EQUALITY AGENDA IN THE 1990s

The Commission on the Status of People with Disabilities was established by the government in 1993. In drawing 60% of its membership from among service users, the Commission exemplified the new way of thinking about disability.

The Commission, chaired by Mr Justice Fergus Flood, toured the country meeting anybody who had anything to say to it including, of course, the various disability groups.

The report of the Commission on the Status of People with Disabilities was wide-ranging in its recommendations but perhaps the most important principle put forward was that services for persons with disabilities should be mainstreamed.[13]

This meant that services for disabled people would be provided by the same organisations that provide a service for everybody else.

Thus, for instance, the training and employment authority FÁS has taken over certain functions of the National Rehabilitation Board.

The health services through the health boards, and more recently through the HSE, remain involved in the provision of life skills programmes and some sheltered services and in other ways.

The Council for the Status of People with Disabilities was established in 1997. It is now known as People with Disabilities in Ireland. Its objective was to be an official body representative of persons with disabilities with the purpose of enabling disabled people to influence public policy and decision-making by public bodies.

The 1990s was a fruitful era in other ways too in terms of the establishment of structures to advance the rights agenda. A Department of Equality and Law Reform was set up in 1997, though it was later subsumed into the Department of Justice, Equality and Law Reform. That Department's Disability Equality Section provides a focal point for disability equality policy and legislation development. The section monitors the implementation of disability mainstreaming policy in relation to public services.

It also administers the funding for the National Disability Authority (see overleaf) which was established in June 2000. In addition, the Section contributes to and monitors progress in the development of international equality policy at European Union, Council of Europe and United Nations levels.[14]

The Forum of People with Disabilities, a non-governmental organisation, lobbies and advocates on behalf of people with disabilities. It was founded in 1990 and played a key role in advancing the disability rights agenda. According to Colgan, it strongly influenced the establishment of the Commission on the Status of People with Disabilities. It also effectively secured the creation of the permanent Council for the Status of People with Disabilities (now People with Disabilities in Ireland, see overleaf).

The adoption of disability issues by the Irish Congress of Trade Unions has also been of significance, according to Colgan. The

ICTU has been able to include disability among the issues addressed during the process of social partnership that has evolved out of the negotiation of national wage agreements.

NEW STRUCTURES AND MEASURES IN THE NEW CENTURY

Two new structures to promote the interests of people with disabilities were set up in 2000.

The National Disability Authority was established on the recommendation of the report of the Commission on the Status of People with Disabilities. The NDA is an independent public body, set up by the National Disability Authority Act, 1999, and funded by the State. The focus of its work is on promoting and securing the rights of people with disabilities. The members of the Authority are persons with disabilities, their representatives, families or carers.

People with Disabilities in Ireland was established with funding from the Department of Justice, Equality and Law Reform as a successor to the Council for the Status of People with Disabilities. Its role is to bring together people with disabilities both nationally and locally to influence decision-making about issues that have an impact on their lives. The organisation links back to county networks made up of people with disabilities.

By 2006 there were, according to an estimate by PDI, almost 400,000 people in Ireland with disabilities of one kind or another —roughly 10% of the population. The 2002 Census showed that 323,707 persons were classified as having a disability i.e. 8.3% of the population.

In recent years, the disability sector has won increasing amounts of funding and support from government. The 2005 Budget, for instance, increased spending on disability by 11%. The purpose of the funding was to provide health services for people with disabilities, to provide further special educational needs, to provide specialised training and employment supports through

FÁS, to pay for reliefs related to disability and to adapt accommodation.[15]

The Citizens Information Board (formerly Comhairle) is the national agency responsible for supporting the provision of information, advice and advocacy on social services. Under the Comhairle Act, 2000, it has been given the task of developing advocacy services. Essentially, these services will enable people with disabilities to obtain their entitlements.

The Disability Act, 2005—a recommendation of the Commission on the Status of People with Disabilities—represents a further step forward for people with disabilities though it has been criticised as not going far enough. However, when fully implemented the Act will entitle disabled persons to obtain from the HSE a statement of their needs and a plan for the provision of these needs. The implementation of the Act will be phased in and in July 2006 the Minister for Health and Children stated that these would be fully phased in by the end of 2011.[16]

RITA LAWLOR

The themes mentioned above are exemplified in the story of Rita Lawlor as told by herself in her book, *Moving On*.[17]

She was born with a learning difficulty in 1957 and after a short period in the local convent school she was sent to a special boarding school in Blackrock, Dublin.

At the age of sixteen she went as a boarder to a convent in Sean McDermott Street. She lived there in the elderly women's section for two years.

At eighteen she began to go to a Rehab training scheme at Rehab's original premises in Pleasants St in Dublin.

Later, she moved to a training workshop run by St Michael's House and later into a hostel run by the same organisation. The setting was semi-independent with a staff member staying overnight.

Gradually she became involved in the Special Olympics where she enjoyed considerable success, winning many medals.

In 1990 she decided, following a week's work experience at the Gresham Hotel in Dublin, that she would not work in a workshop again. She eventually got a job with the Gresham.

It was also in 1990 that she began to become actively involved in rights-based efforts to improve the status of people with disabilities.

She began to go to meetings of the Forum of People with Disabilities. In that same year she and a group of other persons with disabilities established the Dublin City Advocacy Group.

In 1991 she decided that she wanted to live independently on her own and four years later she moved in to her own apartment, built by the Housing Association for Integrated Living (HAIL).

She had begun her involvement with the Special Olympics in 1978. Twenty years later she was one of twelve athletes appointed as global messengers for the Special Olympics.

A key aspect of her story is that health issues figure very little if at all in it. Her focus was on her own self-development. Yet, for much of the period, policy makers saw services for people with disability as belonging to the sphere of health and that attitude changed only slowly.

CONCLUSION

The past 50 years have seen the position of people with disabilities transformed. A segment of the population at high risk of 'disappearing' into the darker corners of the health system half a century ago now asserts its right to participate visibly in society, and society supports that right.

Government has put significant resources into disability services. Disability is no longer seen primarily as a health issue but as one of wider rights in terms of participation in education, employment and social life.

It remains the case, though, that to have a disability is to be severely disadvantaged. In 2005, as many as 13,076 people were still waiting for an assessment for therapeutic intervention and rehabilitation services, according to the Health Research Board's analysis of the National Physical and Sensory Disability Database.[18]

Waiting lists continued for day care and residential care places (Curry, 2003). People with Disabilities in Ireland, in its Budget submission for 2006, pointed out that 2,270 people with intellectual disabilities did not have a service or were missing a major element of service such as a residential service. PDI also pointed out that two thirds of people with a disability had less than 60% level of median income and 22.5% suffered basic deprivation.

Within the health service, a lack of qualified professionals in speech therapy and occupational therapy continued to restrict and hamper the quality of life of persons with disabilities. The PDI submission asked that the restrictions on entry into these professions be dismantled. There were still people staying needlessly in psychiatric hospitals or ordinary hospitals.

And new buildings continued to be built around the country with no access for people with disabilities in spite of building regulations designed to ensure such access, PDI complained.[19]

And the Rehab Group, whose history was outlined earlier, stated on its website in 2006 that, 'even now, there remains a widespread view among the planners of our economy and the controllers of our manpower that people with disabilities have no significant role in generating wealth in Ireland—that they are solely consumers of the social services.'

Nevertheless, as Colgan has pointed out, the past half century has seen an 'extraordinary' growth in the development of services for people with disabilities and the changes in attitudes that have occurred in that time are of at least as great a significance.

Where institutionalisation, sometimes for life, was the norm 50 years ago, accompanied on the occasion by surgery to attempt to reverse the disability, today the thrust of policy is to enable a person with a disability to live at home in his or her own community as a full member of that community.

Chapter 6 ～

FROM COUNTY COUNCIL TO HEALTH SERVICE EXECUTIVE —THE EVOLUTION OF HEALTH ADMINISTRATION

INTRODUCTION

The establishment of the Health Service Executive in 2005 was greeted with little enthusiasm by a public disillusioned by long queues in A&E departments and by lengthy waiting lists for some elective procedures. With the failings of the health system, both real and perceived, the subject of almost daily negative publicity, the creation of a new administrative structure was never likely to be seen as an event to celebrate.

Yet the creation of the HSE was a step of great significance in the evolution of Irish health administration: a point had now been reached at which structures were more simplified than ever before. Of course, whether the simplified structures would deliver health services to an acceptable level of effectiveness remained to be seen.

The HSE replaced seven regional health boards—established under the Health Act, 1970—and the Eastern Regional Health Authority which itself had replaced the Eastern Health Board in 2000. Prior to 1970, there were no fewer than 27 health authorities, made up of county councils and county boroughs. That figure, in turn, represented a significant reduction on the numbers of bodies administering health services at the start of the century.

That said, though, changes in health administration prior to 1970 were modest and incremental compared, for instance, to the establishment of the National Health Service in Britain in 1946. Both economic and political factors account for the slow pace of change.

The economy was poor by European standards. Between 1949 and 1956, real national income was estimated to have risen by only 8% (Ferriter, 2004).[1] In Europe the average was 40%. Emigration was high. Almost 60,000 people left the country in 1958 alone.

The major political factor preventing radical change was the staunch opposition by the Catholic Church to anything that smacked of a welfare state. The failed attempt to introduce free medical treatment for children up to the age of sixteen and for their mothers (known as the Mother and Child Scheme) was a memorable example of that opposition. The controversy led to the resignation in 1952 of the Minister for Health, Dr Noel Browne, following fierce opposition to the scheme from the Catholic Church and the Irish Medical Association.

The health boards administered health services for more than three decades after 1970. As the public grew increasingly dissatisfied with lengthy waiting times in A&E departments in particular, attention turned to what was seen as a cumbersome system of administration.

This dissatisfaction led to the creation of the Health Service Executive which replaced the health boards and a number of other bodies in January 2005.

ORIGINS

The concept of a comprehensive health system administered by a central government is a relatively new one in the social history of Ireland and most other countries. This concept only gradually took hold in Ireland in the late 19th and 20th centuries.

In the early part of the 19th century, as Curry (2003) points out, the authorities were more concerned with preventing a catastrophic spread of infection than they were with promoting good health or even than they were with providing a range of medical services to the sick.[2]

The main hospitals were voluntary, having been set up by charitable organisations, philanthropists or religious orders and were not integrated with any type of overall system. The State's involvement was through county hospitals and fever hospitals, established in the early 19th century; workhouses which came to play an increasingly medical role as the century progressed; and large lunatic asylums, as they were called, and smaller district asylums.

Nevertheless, the century saw the introduction of the rudiments of a health service which continued into comparatively recent times. A dispensary system was introduced under the Poor Relief Act, 1851. The country was divided into dispensary districts and a doctor was employed in each district to provide a free service to poor people in the locality. Those eligible for treatment went to the dispensary to see the doctor who attended on a sessional basis. The system was not replaced until the Choice of Doctor (Medical Card) Scheme was introduced in 1972.[3]

TWENTIETH-CENTURY TRENDS

The first half of the 20th century saw a number of trends which can be said to have led to the development of the health system we have today.

There were four main trends (Curry, 2003):

- First, the health of the individual rather than health of the community became the focus of health policy.
- Second, the role of the State became increasingly important in the provision of health services.
- Third, the huge number of local administrative units was gradually reduced. In the 1920s there were 90 such units. By the

time the VHI was established in 1957 there were fewer than 30. The role of the Department of Health and of central government became increasingly important. A Department of Local Government and Public Health had been established by the Ministers and Secretaries Act, 1924. The Department of Health was established in 1947.

- Fourth, the funding of health services shifted from local taxation to central government. This process continued throughout the period covered by this book and had been completed by the late 1970s.

The establishment of the National Health Service in the United Kingdom may have provided the spur to Irish governments to reform health administration. Northern Ireland was to benefit from the National Health Services Act of 1946 and the government of the Free State was acutely aware of this.[4]

If the reforms mentioned above appear modest by comparison with the development of the National Health Service in the UK, it must be appreciated that, as mentioned earlier, major economic and political obstacles stood in the way of substantial progress. For instance, Ferriter (2004) records that children were being immunised in the 1940s but some doctors, influenced by Catholic social theory, regarded this as an unwarranted interference by the State in the welfare of families.

THE DEPARTMENT OF HEALTH
The Department of Health was established by the Ministers and Secretaries (Amendment) Act, 1946. The new Department's duties included the prevention and cure of disease; the treatment and care of persons suffering from physical defects and mental illness; the initiation and direction of research; the regulation of areas such as the training and registration of persons for the health services; and control of proprietary medical and toilet preparations.

The inauguration of the Department can be seen as the first major step towards the development of a modern, comprehensive health service in Ireland. It could be argued that the second major step was not taken until 1970 and the third until 2005.

According to Jerry O'Dwyer, a former secretary of the Department of Health, a White Paper[5] on health published in 1947 represented a significant achievement for the politicians and the civil servants who promoted the policies contained in it (O'Dwyer, 1997).[6] Most significantly, the White Paper proposed that eligibility for health services should gradually be extended to the entire population. It took until 1991 for this to be fully achieved.

Despite the establishment of the Department of Health, the administration of health services at local level was undertaken not by dedicated health bodies but by county councils and county boroughs. This was copperfastened by the Health Acts of 1947 and 1953. While these bodies were known as 'health authorities', no separate authorities were legally constituted for this purpose (Henscy, 1979). In 1959 consultative health committees were set up to advise the city and county managers on the operation of the general health services.

Mental hospitals were treated differently and were governed by special joint boards operating under the Mental Treatment Act, 1945.

THE CREATION OF A MODERN HEALTH ADMINISTRATION
Dáil Select Committee 1962–65 and the 1966 White Paper
The establishment of what we would now see as a modern health administration had its origins in the work of a Dáil Select Committee which sat from 1962 to 1965 and in the ensuing 1966 White Paper.[7]

A number of developments made change necessary (Curry, 2003). The cost of financing the health services had long been beyond the means of local authorities and had been almost entirely taken over by the central government. Many hospital services were no longer provided purely on a county basis so that it became necessary to organise the services in a way which transcended county borders. Separating health services from local authorities was a logical follow-on from the establishment of the Department of Health. The White Paper published in 1947 had recognised this and had suggested that health services might be coordinated on a regional basis. This happened—23 years later.

The White Paper led to the introduction of the Choice of Doctor Scheme and the establishment of eight regional health boards to take over the running of public health services from the local authorities.

Though the White Paper was pivotal in moving the adminis-tration of health services in Ireland into the modern era, its authors were insistent that it was not doing anything radical.

O'Dwyer (1979) notes that the White Paper made it clear the State was under no obligation to provide health services free of charge for everyone. There was to be no NHS in Ireland. However, it did lay down another interesting principle which was that nobody should be obliged to show dire need before being able to avail of a health service.[8]

Commission of Inquiry on Mental Illness, 1966

As mentioned above, the administration of mental health services was separate from that of the rest of the health service. The 1966 *Report of the Commission of Inquiry on Mental Illness*[9] sought to bring this, too, into the modern era. The Commission's report envisaged a move away from the use of psychiatric hospitals towards the development of community services, the provision of psychiatric units in general hospitals and other modernising measures. However, as Walsh (1997) has commented, the Commission did not discuss how, organisationally, these changes would be brought about and this blunted the impact of its recommendations.[10]

The health boards

The 27 health authorities which had administered health services locally were replaced by eight regional health boards from 1 April 1971. The eight health boards were:

The Eastern Health Board, covering Dublin, Kildare and Wicklow.

The Mid Western Health Board, covering Limerick, Clare and Tipperary North.

The Midland Health Board, covering Laois, Longford, Offaly and Westmeath.

The North Eastern Health Board, covering Cavan, Louth, Meath and Monaghan.

The North Western Health Board, covering Donegal, Leitrim and Sligo.

The South Eastern Health Board, covering Carlow, Kilkenny, Tipperary South, Waterford and Wexford.

The Southern Health Board, covering Cork and Kerry.

The Western Health Board, covering Galway, Mayo and Roscommon.

The board of each health board had a majority of members made up of local elected representatives. Other members represented professional interests such as doctors, nurses, dentists and pharmacists. Each board had three members nominated by the Minister for Health.

The work of the health boards was organised in three 'programmes': community care, general hospitals and special hospitals.

The community care programme covered three areas of work: community protection, community health services and community welfare. Community protection included public health functions such as immunisation, health promotion and prevention of infectious diseases. Community health services included GP services, home nursing and other services provided outside a hospital setting. Community welfare comprised the making of cash payments, grants to voluntary bodies, administration of home help services and child care services.

The general hospitals programme was responsible for the treatment of patients in health board hospitals or, under contract, in voluntary or private hospitals.

The special hospitals programme dealt with services for persons with psychiatric illnesses, for persons with intellectual disabilities and for persons requiring geriatric services.

Despite modernisation, old ways of thinking, and of treating people, persisted. Viney (1969) noted that the County Homes—many of which today are long-stay hospitals—had still not shaken off 'the workhouse mode of thought' and that those who lived in them were regarded in many communities as social pariahs.[11]

Choice of doctor scheme

The dispensary system, which had persisted since the 19th century, came to an end in 1972 with the implementation of the Choice of Doctor Scheme. Under the Scheme, persons who passed the means test, and certain other categories of people, became entitled to a free GP service, free prescribed medicines and a free public ward hospital service. Treatment was to be provided in the GP's own surgery using the same facilities as those afforded to the doctor's private patients. This development removed the stigma which had attached to attending a dispensary.

Local health committees

The Health Act, 1970, also provided for the establishment of local advisory committees. These were made up of such people as elected representatives, county council officials, doctors and representatives of voluntary bodies. The committees were there to advise the health boards but whether they had any particular influence is unclear and they were abolished in 1988.

REPORTS AND STRATEGIES

Following the implementation of changes brought about by the Health Act, 1970, a series of reports and government strategies paved the way for further developments, though sometimes many years elapsed between recommendation and implementation. The main documents are mentioned below:

The Commission on Health Funding

The Commission on Health Funding was set up in 1987 at a time of deep cuts in health services. It reported in 1989. The Commission's recommendations concerning funding are referred to elsewhere.[12] The Commission recommended that the Department of Health disengage from any involvement in the management of health services. For instance, the Department should cease to fund voluntary hospitals directly. Instead, the Department should be a policy-making body. The health boards should be abolished and replaced by a single Health Services Executive Authority. It was to take a decade and a half for these recommendations to be implemented with the establishment of the Health Service Executive under the Health Act, 2004.[13]

Planning for the Future, 1984

As noted earlier, the 1966 *Report of the Commission of Inquiry on Mental Illness* failed to outline how, in an organisational way, the psychiatric services might be improved so as to reduce the high rates of admission to psychiatric hospitals. The 1984 report, *The*

Psychiatric Services: Planning for the Future, rectified this omission. It suggested that psychiatric institutions be replaced with psychiatric wards in general hospitals and that community-based services be improved and developed. As described elsewhere, progress was patchy and slow. Nevertheless, *Planning for the Future* provided the template which has been followed, however unsatisfactorily, to bring psychiatric services into the modern age.[14]

Shaping a Healthier Future, 1994

Health gain and social gain were the two key concepts in the 1994 strategy (Curry, 2003). What this meant was health planners should focus on achieving positive outcomes for patients rather than simply focusing on the level of service or the amount of services provided. Wellbeing and not the absence of disease should be the criterion for the provision of health services.[15]

Underlying the strategy were three stated principles: equity, equality and accountability. As O'Dwyer (1997) put it, these principles were to be the 'sheet anchor' of the strategy. The strategy also signalled a change in direction for the Department of Health. The Department was seen as primarily a strategic planning body working in partnership with the health boards and with other bodies providing healthcare. According to O'Dwyer the 1994 strategy represented 'a key event, a major change in official thinking about planning and managing the health services in Ireland.'[16]

Changing the role of the Department of Health

The process of changing the role of the Department of Health from one of direct involvement with services to a strategic, policy role was given legislative authority by the Health (Amendment) (Number 3) Act, 1996. Among other measures, this legislation transferred the funding of voluntary public hospitals and of the main organisations for people with intellectual disabilities from the Department of Health to the health boards. This change was implemented in 1998. The Department had been re-named the Department of Health and Children in 1997.

The Eastern Regional Health Authority

In 2000, the Eastern Regional Health Authority replaced the former Eastern Health Board. Three Area Health Boards were established within the ERHA region. These were the East Coast Area Health Board, the Northern Area Health Board and the South Western Area Health Board. The ERHA was closely involved with the work of the Area Health Boards, and monitored and evaluated the services provided by them.

The ERHA came to be seen as exemplifying the phenomenon of excessive administration in the health services. Where there had been one organisation—the Eastern Health Board—there were now five: the ERHA itself, the three Area Health Boards and the ERHA Shared Services (the latter provided personnel and other services to the ERHA). One Director of Nursing complained to the author that while her hospital had previously applied for funding to the Department of Health and Children, it had now to apply to the Area Health Board which brought the application to the ERHA which then might bring the application to the Department. From her perspective, the establishment of the ERHA had made health provision at a local level more complicated than before.

Quality and Fairness, A Health System for You, 2001

The 2001 health strategy[17] was undertaken in response to public criticism of the health service. The economy had undergone a sea change. Following more than a decade of economic difficulty and cutbacks, new jobs had been created at the rate of more than a thousand a week from the mid-1990s to 2000 (Ferriter, 2004).

But waiting lists for surgery were long, and delays and poor conditions in A&E departments began to reach critical levels from the viewpoint of the public and of hospital staff.[18]

The health strategy envisaged the provision of 3,000 extra public beds by 2011. It provided for the establishment of the National Treatment Purchase Fund to pay for public patients to be treated in private hospitals in Ireland and in the UK. It envisaged an expansion and development of GP services.

It envisaged the establishment of a Health Service Executive, the abolition of the health boards and a reduction in the number of health agencies.

The Department of Health and Children appointed Prospectus Management Consultants in 2002 to review health structures and to make recommendations, in the light of what the strategy had proposed. The outline of future structures contained in the Prospectus report—*Audit of Structures and Functions in the Health System* (2003)[19]—is essentially the system that was implemented and that exists today.

Mental Health Act, 2001
The main thrust of the Mental Health Act, 2001, was to protect the rights of persons involuntarily admitted to psychiatric hospitals. The Act led to the establishment of the Mental Health Commission which has two roles: to ensure the implementation of the Mental Health Act and to ensure that modern, high-quality systems of care are introduced into the psychiatric services.

Regional Health Forums
Four Regional Health Forums were established, under the Health Act, 2004, to give politicians a voice, of sorts, in relation to health services. Local politicians had criticised their exclusion from the board of the Health Service Executive. The Regional Health Forums give them at least the appearance of involvement.

THE HEALTH SERVICE EXECUTIVE AND OTHER DEVELOPMENTS IN CURRENT HEALTH ADMINISTRATION

The HSE

The Health Service Executive came into operation in January 2005. It was made up of three main sections: a National Hospitals Office, a Primary Community and Continuing Care Directorate, and the National Shared Services Centre. The National Hospitals Office administers hospital services nationally. The Primary Community and Continuing Care Directorate has responsibility for non-hospital services in the community. The way in which the Directorate and the National Hospitals Office work together will be crucial to the success of the HSE—for example, the discharge of patients from hospital will impact on the work both of the Directorate and of the National Hospitals Office. The National Shared Services Centre is responsible for payroll, personnel and similar functions.

Many existing bodies were subsumed into the HSE. Apart from the regional health boards these include the Health Service Employers Agency, the Health Boards Executive, the Office for Health Management, Comhairle na nOspidéal, the General Medical Services (Payments) Board, the National Disease Surveillance Centre and the Hospital Bodies Administration Bureau.

Health Information and Quality Authority

Though it received little public attention or comment, one of the most important bodies set up as part of the health reform programme was the Health Information and Quality Authority.

The overall aim of the Authority, as outlined by the Minister for Health and Children, Mary Harney TD, in January 2005,[20] is to advance the aim of delivering high-quality services that are based on evidence-supported best practice. This in turn is a key policy aim of the Health Strategy.

The responsibilities of the Authority are built around three functions: developing health information; promoting and implementing quality assurance programmes nationally; and overseeing health technology assessment.

An interim board was appointed to the Authority in January 2005.

STATUTORY COMPLAINTS SYSTEM

Regulations to implement a statutory complaints system from 1 January 2007 were made by the Minister for Health and Children, Mary Harney TD, in 2006. Under the system, a complaint will be investigated by a complaints officer appointed by the HSE or service provider, as appropriate; the complainant may request a review of any recommendation made by a complaints officer; and reviews will be carried out by a review officer appointed by the Executive or a person to whom the Executive has assigned its review functions. Separately, and independently, a complainant is also entitled, under the framework, to refer his or her complaint to the Ombudsman or Ombudsman for Children, as appropriate, where he or she is dissatisfied with the recommendation made or any of the steps taken by the Executive or service provider in relation to the complaint.[21]

PRIVATE HEALTHCARE

The administration of private healthcare has largely been left to its providers. There are indications, however, that the State, through its agencies, will become increasingly involved in this area and this is dealt with in more detail in Part Two.

Public involvement in the administration of private health has been more in the nature of indirect influence than direct involvement. For instance, the regulations covering the Choice of Doctor Scheme, introduced in 1972, stipulate that the facilities offered to public patients i.e. medical card patients must be the same as those offered to private patients.

The term 'private healthcare' in Ireland is frequently taken to mean healthcare in private hospitals. Again there has been no unified system of administration of private hospitals during the period.

In recent years, however, the involvement of the State in private healthcare has increased. The major example of this is the establishment of the National Treatment Purchase Fund as a result of the 2001 health strategy. The fund, in providing for treatment in private hospitals of patients on the public waiting list, directly affects the financing of private hospitals and thereby may indirectly influence the configuration of those hospitals.

This, however, can hardly be described as an involvement in administration. Similarly, monies paid by the VHI for the treatment of patients in private hospitals have constituted the major source of funding for these hospitals but this does not represent an involvement in administration.

It is worth noting that the State imposes no licensing requirements on hospitals although such a requirement exists for other areas such as pubs! There is a huge need for active State involvement in this area to ensure quality standards for new and existing hospitals perhaps through a formal accreditation service, according to Dr Bernadette Carr, Medical Director, Vhi Healthcare. Such accreditation might also provide an indication of the casemix capable of being handled at each hospital e.g. high-tech procedures (cardiac/oncology); general surgery and medical; and even bumps and bruises.

CONCLUSION

In 50 years, we have moved from having many health authorities—usually on a county basis—to having one overall health authority, the Health Service Executive. Health service administrators face higher expectations than ever before from the public. While medical advances have brought the possibilities of successful treatment to unprecedented levels, it seems fair to say that administrative advances have lagged behind. Nevertheless, it must be acknowledged that the past half century has seen a sea change in administrative structures. We do not know whether the new structure will work—but at least we have seen that administrative systems have a capacity for change and that, in itself, is a source of optimism.

Chapter 7 ⌒

THE MEDICAL AND NURSING PROFESSIONS

INTRODUCTION

The histories of the medical and nursing professions in Ireland display sharp contrasts. Doctors have been jealous of their independence while nurses, trained until this century in a hierarchical, apprenticeship system, were expected to give almost unquestioning obedience. Doctors have been willing to fight, throughout the period, on issues concerning their income; nurses did not do so for many decades. Doctors have traditionally been anxious to protect their right to private practice; nurses have usually been salaried employees.

In the accounts that follow, the author has drawn heavily on Ruth Barrington's *Health, Medicine & Politics in Ireland 1900–1970* (Institute of Public Administration, Dublin, 1987) and on the *Report of the Commission on Nursing, a blueprint for the future* (Stationery Office, Dublin, 1998).

DOCTORS
The period to 1932

At the start of the 20th century, hospitals were for the poor. Those who could afford to pay were treated in their own homes. Voluntary hospitals, mainly in Dublin, provided a free service for the very poor. The hospital system outside Dublin was little developed. Local authority hospitals had their origins in the infirmaries attached to workhouses and the standard of care often reflected this. For the poor, a GP service was provided from district dispensaries. In Dublin, some who could afford to do so joined friendly societies which paid for their GP services.

This was the context within which doctors worked.

The dispensaries were created in 1851, a development promoted by a surgeon, Denis Phelan, who was also an Assistant Poor Law Commissioner. He based the idea for dispensaries run by local authorities on dispensaries which landlords had financed for their tenants earlier in the century.

Each dispensary doctor was employed by a Board of Guardians and was entitled to engage in private as well as public practice. Some supplemented their income also by acting as medical officers for local workhouses.

By the beginning of the 20th century there were 800 dispensary doctors and they comprised about one third of all registered medical practitioners in Ireland. Salaries and conditions appear to have been relatively poor and whether a doctor would get a pension was at the discretion of the Board of Guardians.

The doctor saw private patients in his own house—the better off feared they might be infected by close contact with the poor.

The Irish Medical Association, like its counterpart the British Medical Association, was founded in the 1830s. Its main focus was on dispensary doctors or doctors working as the medical officers of workhouses or lunatic asylums. But its attempts to improve salaries by encouraging doctors to refuse to apply for posts which paid rates less than those the Association considered the minimum were often unsuccessful. Candidates applied even for the more poorly paid posts. For many years the Association languished but it was to become a major force in the great controversies of the 1940s and 1950s.

The British Medical Association in Ireland had quite a different focus as its members tended to be specialists or other doctors whose income was derived entirely from private practice.

The dispensaries were bleak places and there was a stigma attached to attending them. Yet they appear to have provided a level of medical service to the poor which perhaps was lacking in England at that time. The Royal Commission on the Poor Laws, appointed in 1905, noted that public spending on salaries for doctors and on drugs in Ireland was more than half the equivalent in England.[1]

Conflict arising out of doctors' fears that proposals to extend eligibility for medical services would reduce their income and independence has been a feature of the relationship between doctors and the State for at least a century.

One of the earliest of these conflicts concerned an attempt to provide medical benefits for insured workers whose doctors would, under the plan, be paid out of national insurance contributions.

In a lengthy campaign, doctors successfully opposed the measure. One result of this was that the dispensary system, with all the stigma attached to it, continued until 1972.

The proposed arrangement seems to have been opposed by doctors partly because they disliked the concept of working under contract to insurance companies and partly because they were unhappy with being paid under a capitation scheme.

Some doctors who did not wish to be on the insurance company panels themselves nevertheless feared that they would lose patients to doctors who might join such panels and they also opposed the scheme.

A new echelon of publicly-paid doctors was created by the Local Government Act, 1925, which provided for the appointment of County Medical Officers of Health to oversee public health activities such as the implementation of the laws on sanitation. Their salaries, however, had to be paid out of local rates and therefore the spread of the network of County Medical Officers of Health was relatively slow. Nevertheless, the advent of County Medical Officers of Health saw the development of such services as medical inspection of children in the national schools. The latter had been provided for since 1919 but little had been done to implement inspections.

The 1930s and 1940s

The Fianna Fáil government elected in 1932 appointed Seán T. Ó Ceallaigh TD as Minister for Local Government and Public Health and Dr F.C. Ward TD as his Parliamentary Secretary, a post similar to that of Minister of State or Junior Minister today.

Dr Ward, who had been a dispensary doctor, was, in effect, given the health portfolio. But like another doctor who was later given the portfolio—Noel Browne TD—he had a talent for alienating people. Those he alienated included his fellow doctors and this was to lead to his downfall.

Nevertheless, Ward was one of the major figures in the development of the health services. He expanded public health measures including school medical examinations and increased the number of public hospitals built with money raised by the Irish Hospital Sweepstakes.

But he managed to alienate quite a remarkable range of doctors. Barrington outlines them as follows:

- Ward's egalitarian views made doctors in the voluntary hospitals fearful that their own private practice would suffer as public hospitals were built outside Dublin and as Ward reduced the autonomy of the voluntary hospitals. These consultants were not paid for treating public patients and depended on private practice for their incomes.
- Dispensary doctors were upset because their service was neglected and was deprived of funding from the Sweepstakes.

Nor would Ward agree to increase their salaries. Also, Ward was diligent in rooting out abuses among dispensary doctors.

- Ward had a dispute with the Irish Medical Association concerning fees for diphtheria immunisation which resulted in much bad feeling.
- He angered county surgeons by attempting to limit their ability to engage in private practice.

That doctors did not agree with many of his initiatives was not necessarily significant in itself—in much of what he did he was motivated by egalitarian principles. But where a mixture of diplomacy and determination was required, Ward exacerbated his opposition by his undiplomatic manner.

During Ward's time, doctors dropped their demand for the dispensary system to be run by a national agency rather than by local authorities and Ward's abrasiveness may have contributed to this.

Debate on the future of the health services was a feature of the 1940s and the Irish Medical Association represented the interest of doctors in this debate, though not always with a united voice.

For instance, the IMA failed to support proposals put forward by its president Dr John Shanley who had been a Poor Law medical officer in Dublin and was very familiar with the health needs of the poor.

In 1944, he proposed that a Minister for Health be appointed who would work through an executive body administering public health services in four regions. Everybody with an income below £550 pounds would be entitled to 'a complete and efficient medical service, including consultant, specialist and hospital treatment free of at least direct payment'.

Doctors would be paid a capitation fee and the service would be financed by insurance contributions, by the rates and by the Exchequer.

Dr Shanley had put the proposals forward without having them accepted by the IMA. In December 1944 the IMA published proposals which rowed back from Shanley's vision. The IMA scheme would, among other things, exclude maternity treatment from the free medical service. Instead of being seen by doctors on a capitation rate, those eligible would attend the dispensary. The means test would exclude more people than that proposed by Shanley. The salaries of dispensary doctors would be increased.

The IMA scheme was criticised in the media as one devised for doctors rather than patients.

A new medical influence arrived at the Department of Local Government and Public Health in 1944 when Dr James Deeny, a GP, was appointed Chief Medical Officer. He was an exceptionally energetic man who can take much of the credit for ending the scourge of TB as a devastating illness. Deeny invested in sanatoria and provided for the employment of more thoracic surgeons and other professionals. Doctors and other staff were sent abroad to study methods of treatment. The credit for Dr Deeny's work went to Dr Noel Browne, who became Minister for Health in 1948.[2]

Meanwhile, Dr Ward continued to alienate the medical profession by refusing to consult with them about a new health bill. Finally a former president of the Irish Medical Association, Dr Patrick MacCarvill, sent a series of allegations to the Taoiseach Mr de Valera concerning Dr Ward. The allegations turned out to have no foundation except for one—that he had not made a complete tax return for his bacon business. Ward resigned.

The IMA had been determined that Ward would not become Minister for Health and had even organised a collection to meet any legal expenses that might be incurred by Dr MacCarvill as a result of making his allegations.

Now a new threat arose, from the perspective of the IMA, in the form of a proposal for a new medical service put forward by the Minister for Health, Seán MacEntee TD. The plan, if implemented, would make a free GP service available to about 75% of the population. 'It is small consolation for a patient to realise that we have in this country great men in medicine—if that same patient is unable through a lack of means or organisation to secure their services,' Mr MacEntee told the IMA in 1946.[3]

But opposition to the plan soon arose within the Irish Medical Association. The charge was led by County Medical Officer in Limerick, Dr James McPolin and by his colleagues. McPolin and his supporters appealed to Catholic doctrine, arguing that the concept of a State medical service was in breach of the moral law and impinged on the duty of the family to care for its own children. These views were later to be central to the bitter controversy over the Mother and Child Scheme.

Dr McPolin and his Limerick colleagues also attacked the concept of compulsory medical inspections, seen by the drafters of the Bill as a public health issue. It is interesting to note that prior to the eruption of the controversy the Department of Local Government and Public Health had been so concerned at the poor state of preventive health services under Dr McPolin in Limerick that it had contemplated suspending him.

This opposition, combined with the opposition of Fine Gael and the bishops, led to a serious scaling down of the proposals for a free medical service but in 1948 Fianna Fáil was defeated in a general election and a coalition government, led by Fine Gael which opposed the extension of free medical services, took power. By now there was a separate Department of Health, instituted in 1947 with Dr James Ryan TD, a non-practising medical doctor, as Minister. Ryan was succeeded in 1948 by Dr Noel Browne TD. Under the new government, as mentioned elsewhere, controversy over the Mother and Child Scheme (see overleaf) continued but ultimately Browne, with little support from his colleagues, resigned. A much watered-down version was introduced by the next Fianna Fáil government.

As with Dr Ward, Dr Browne appears to have had no compunction about alienating the medical profession and many others he came in contact with. As with Ward also, Browne's policies were often forward looking but his abrasive personality magnified the opposition to these policies.

Sources of contention between Dr Browne and the IMA were plentiful.

For instance, there was a dispute between Browne and the Irish Medical Association over Browne's desire to introduce medical cards so that the poor would not need to apply for a ticket every time they wanted to go to the dispensary. Neither would they agree to Browne's proposal that persons with medical cards should be seen in the same surgery as private patients. Neither of these measures would be introduced until the 1970s.

When the newspapers carried an advertisement from Browne saying that any complaints patients might have regarding a dispensary doctor would be transmitted to him within 24 hours, the result was, naturally enough, to alienate dispensary doctors.

Browne also publicly criticised the consultants for what he saw as their excessive interest in money.

And changes in the funding of voluntary hospitals meant that they would have to treat increasing numbers of poor people in order to maintain their income. These changes greatly angered consultants in Dublin.

The Mother and Child Scheme[4] which proposed a free medical service for children up to the age of sixteen threatened consultants' income and the private income of GPs. As mentioned earlier, consultants derived their income from treating paying patients and were generally not paid for treating poorer patients. By greatly increasing the number of patients who would be treated at no cost, the Minister was reducing their customer base. At the other end of the scale, dispensary doctors feared their surgeries would be flooded with patients and disliked the possibility that the better off might have to share waiting rooms with the poor.

The Irish Medical Association and the hierarchy continued with their attack on the Mother and Child Scheme. The Irish

Medical Association in 1951 suggested that the scheme be means-tested and that mothers whose income was below the means test limit should receive a cash grant which they could then spend on maternity medical services. The IMA also advertised in the national newspapers objecting to what it claimed was politically controlled medicine. By now the pressure from the hierarchy was intense. The Cabinet was unwilling to oppose the bishops and Dr Browne was left with no option but to resign. The Mother and Child Scheme as originally proposed and the extension of free GP services to 75% of the population had been fought off by the doctors and the bishops.

Shortly afterwards, the IMA found itself very briefly at the centre of policy-making when the Taoiseach, Mr Costello, set up a committee made up of IMA representatives, departmental medical officers and the acting Chief Medical Officer to devise a new mother and child scheme which would 'fully respect the Catholic social teaching in regard to the individual and society'.[5] But the government quickly fell and both the doctors and the bishops found themselves under attack in the subsequent general election which was won by Fianna Fáil. On his return as Minister for Health, Dr James Ryan dissolved the committee.

The 1950s
Dr Ryan was determined to press ahead with the Mother and Child Scheme. By contrast with Dr Browne, however, he avoided creating unnecessary confrontation. He assured the IMA that he was not interested in providing 'a complete scheme of state medicine' and he asked the IMA for its views about how services might be improved.

The Mother and Child Scheme would now cover children up to the age of six. Even this required skilful negotiation with the doctors and bishops by Dr Ryan, backed by the Taoiseach Mr de Valera.

The government also legislated successfully for an extension of entitlement to free hospital services. As part of this move, consultants in voluntary hospitals would be paid directly by the health authorities for treating patients eligible for hospital services.

A coalition government succeeded Fianna Fáil in 1954 but Ryan had seen to it that the Health Act, 1953, was signed into law before the election. The new government was led by Fine Gael and supported by the Labour Party, and the latter was in support of the Act which was brought into operation over a two-year period. In talks with the Irish Medical Association the new Minister for Health, T.F. O'Higgins TD, agreed to set up a body to look into the feasibility of establishing a voluntary health insurance scheme. The work of this body led to the establishment of the Voluntary Health Insurance Board in 1957.

Mr O'Higgins also agreed to allow county surgeons to have a private practice and to greater autonomy for the Medical Registration Council (predecessor to the Medical Council).

A period of conflict, negotiation and compromise drew to a close. As Barrington puts it, the effect of all of these measures was to greatly reduce the chances for ordinary Irish people of dying from infectious disease, of TB, of complications of childbirth or of suffering disabling but treatable diseases.

The health service had been significantly improved and a combination of eligibility for hospital services for most of the population and the establishment of the VHI for people in the higher income groups meant that medical costs need no longer be feared by anybody.

The medical profession had managed to preserve the right of doctors in local authority hospitals to engage in private practice. In concert with the bishops, the doctors had managed to prevent the extension of a free GP service to most of the population. Nevertheless, the government had succeeded in bringing about a major modernisation and improvement of health services.

Moreover, the Mother and Child Scheme foreshadowed the present Medical Card Scheme in the sense that mothers had a choice of which doctor they would attend for maternity care—they did not have to attend the dispensary doctors. This arrangement became popular with both patients and doctors.

While an era of major conflict had ended, all was not plain sailing for the Irish Medical Association in its relations with government, though. Seán MacEntee TD became Minister for Health when Fianna Fáil returned to government in 1957. Relations between himself and the Irish Medical Association were poor, to say the least.

A dispute broke out between the Association and the Minister concerning the Minister's right to see patient records where a complaint had been made against a dispensary doctor. Moreover, the Minister would not accept the Irish Medical Association as a negotiator under the Trade Union Act, 1941.

The Association retaliated by instructing its members not to apply for public medical posts. When the Minister addressed the annual conference of the Irish Medical Association in Killarney in 1959 he asked the IMA to cease attempting to block applications for public posts.

But the IMA continued to advise members not to apply and the Minister expressed his displeasure by sending it a cheque for £5 to cover the cost of his dinner and that of his wife in Killarney. This resulted in an attack on MacEntee and his wife in the IMA *Journal* which attacked him for sending a cheque 'to cover the expense of the entertainment of himself and his formidable escort.'[6]

From that point on, he would have nothing to do with the IMA.

It was not until 1963 that the issues between the IMA and the Minister were settled. It was agreed that an Irish Medical Union would be set up to negotiate pay and conditions. In 1984, the IMA and the IMU were amalgamated to form the Irish Medical Organisation with trade union negotiating rights.

Brown and Chadwick (1997) note that the 1950s saw a transition from a system in which private medicine and charity predominated to one in which the majority of the population had an entitlement to hospital services.[7]

The 1960s

In the 1960s and in light of the experience of the choice of doctor element of the Mother and Child Scheme, the feasibility of establishing a choice of doctor scheme in place of the dispensary services was examined by a committee chaired by Brendan Hensey, later to become Secretary of the Department of Health. The committee's report, completed in 1962 and not published, suggested a choice of doctor scheme (Barrington, 1987) similar to that in operation today—but it would be ten years before the old dispensary system ended and a choice of doctor scheme was implemented.[8]

The concept of a choice of doctor and of the payment of doctors by capitation was repeated in the 1966 White Paper. While the Choice of Doctor Scheme began in 1972, the medical profession insisted on payment of a fee per item of service and capitation was not introduced until 1989.

Barrington (1987) notes that by the end of the 1960s hostilities had died away and the Health Act, 1970, demonstrated 'a virtual alliance of interest' between the doctors, the Minister for Health and the Department.

A major opportunity for the medical profession to influence the health services came with the establishment of the Fitzgerald Committee. The Consultative Council on General Hospital Services was established in 1967. Its chairman, Professor Patrick Fitzgerald, was a professor of surgery at University College Dublin. All its members were consultants, some with local health authority hospitals and some with voluntary hospitals.

Its proposals,[9] as Barrington points out, were reminiscent of those made by the Hospitals Commission in the 1930s. They foreshadowed those of the Hanly Report in 2003.

The proposals are summarised in Chapter Two but they envisaged a system based on four regional hospitals and nine general hospitals. Needless to say, the opposition from local communities, concerned at the 'downgrading' of their hospitals, was immediate and fiery and the report—based on the views of the medical profession—remained unimplemented.

1970 to 2006

Brown and Chadwick[10] point out that the 1970s, when the major recommendations of the 1966 White Paper were implemented and the health boards were formed, brought doctors more closely into the business of creating policy through their membership of health boards, Comhairle na nOspidéal and other bodies. The period since 1970 has seen its share of controversy between doctors and the State but none that compares with the battles of the previous era.

This period has seen the commencement of the modernisation of general practice which, in Ireland, evolved from the dispensary system. That system meant not only that every district in the country had a doctor to provide services to the very poor but also that every district had a doctor who could provide private services to the those were not poor—and it was very often the same doctor.

The implementation of the Choice of Doctor Scheme in 1972 brought the dispensary system to an end. From this point onwards, GPs worked under contract in treating patients with medical cards.

A major advance in the position of general practice came in 1984 when the Irish College of General Practitioners was inaugurated. With the support of almost every GP in the country, the College instituted training programmes, research and continuing education work. In 1997, the College opened a Postgraduate Resource Centre. One outcome of the work of the ICGP has been the growth in the proportion of GPs who have undergone a three-year, formal training programme in general practice. In 1982, only 9% of GPs had undergone such training but by 2005, 36% of GPs had done so and almost every doctor entering general practice was vocationally trained,[11] according to a presentation to the Irish College of General Practitioners by Professor Tom O'Dowd, Professor of General Practice, Trinity College Dublin.

Boland (1997) refers to a survey of Irish general practice conducted by the College in 1996.[12] The survey identified 2,200 GPs, a number little changed, as it happens, over the previous hundred years with an average of 1,635 patients per GP.

Some tensions exist between GPs and hospitals. Boland (1997) notes, for example, that GPs are frustrated by a system whereby patients referred to the hospitals by them must be screened in A&E departments by doctors who have less experience than the GPs who originally referred them.

As detailed elsewhere,[13] the 2001 health strategy envisaged a new status for GPs as part of a wider primary care service. The strategy saw primary care as 'the central focus of the delivery of health and personal social services in Ireland.'

It envisaged that primary care would be delivered by teams which would include 'GPs, nurses/midwives, healthcare assistants, home helps, physiotherapists, occupational therapists, social workers and administrative personnel. A wider primary care network of other primary care professionals such as speech and language therapists, community pharmacists, dieticians, community welfare officers, dentists, chiropodists and psychologists will also provide services for the enrolled population of each primary care team.'

In the autumn of 2006, the HSE said it would establish 500 primary care teams across the country in the next four years.[14]

As noted elsewhere,[15] an attempt by the Minister for Health, Brendan Corish TD, to provide an entitlement to free hospital services to all from 1974 was frustrated by the opposition of consultants who believed that such a move would have an adverse effect on their income and conditions of employment (Curry,

2003).[16] Ferriter (2004) remarks that by now the consultants were able to win the battle 'without the support of the Catholic hierarchy, unlike previously.'[17]

In 1979 eligibility for hospital services was broadened but there still remained a group of people on the higher income levels who were expected to pay for specialist services even in a public ward. This was eliminated in 1991, almost twenty years after the attempt by Corish to bring in such a system.

The health cuts of the 1980s, which substantially reduced the number of hospital beds in the system, also protected the position of private practice as more persons joined the VHI to ensure they could obtain treatment within a reasonable period of time.

However, there was also criticism of consultants who were seen to spend time doing private work which should have been spent fulfilling their contractual duties to public patients. The *Value for Money Audit of the Irish Health System* (2001) commissioned by the Department of Health and Children acknowledged these criticisms but found no systematic evidence to support them, though it accepted it lacked full information to enable it to assess the situation. It says:

> In our discussions with Board managers and hospital managers, we found widespread concern that the private healthcare system is reducing the resources available for public healthcare. This is particularly seen as being due to consultants spending more time on private healthcare than is appropriate within their contract.
>
> However, we have identified no systematic evidence to support any widespread abuse of public sector responsibilities by consultants. The lack of hard evidence on the amount of activity in the private sector carried out by individual consultants does, however, hinder the making of informed judgments on the issue.[18]

A consultants' contract, negotiated in 1981, gave consultants employment as pensionable public servants with a requirement that they work 33 hours per week. It also gave them a right to unlimited private practice. In 1991, when eligibility for free public hospital services was extended to the entire population, 20% of public hospital beds were designated for private patients.

An analysis by Brown of quantitative research with 29 consultants in public voluntary hospitals in the late 1990s gives an interesting insight into the views of consultants at that time.[19] Findings included:

- Consultants identified strongly with the hospitals in which they worked and with the traditions of those hospitals.
- Their loyalty was to the hospital and not the Department of Health.
- Consultants were opposed to any measures which might reduce the independence of their hospitals and their freedom to develop new services.
- Consultants had a very good opinion of hospital managers with whom they strongly identified. Almost all consultants wanted the mixture of public and private practice to continue. They argued that the mix removed some of the burden from the public system, that it brought income into the public system through VHI payments and that public-private mix helped to safeguard consultants' autonomy.
- Private practice, they argued, strengthened a sense of vocation among consultants.
- They believed that most consultants worked more than the hours to which they were committed under the public contract and that therefore there was little abuse of the private system. Nevertheless they did see a need for the balance between public and private beds to be monitored to ensure that it remained fair and to ensure the private practice did not reach the stage where it might be harmful to the public system. And they

accepted that some consultants had a greater interest in private than in public practice.

Doctors, through the Irish Medical Organisation, also opposed the decision to make every person over 70, regardless of income, eligible for a medical card from July 2001. A substantial number of persons over that age was already entitled to the medical card but the IMO argued unsuccessfully that the government plan would extend medical cards to those who did not need them at the expense of persons at the other end of the scale whose income put them just over the limit for eligibility. Ultimately, however, the medical cards were extended to everybody aged over 70 with doctors agreeing to accept a substantially higher capitation fee for the private patients that they would now lose.

The IMO represents registered medical practitioners in all areas of work. The Irish Hospital Consultants Association represents most consultants.

The Medical Council was formed following the passing of the Medical Practitioners Act in 1978. The primary duty of the Medical Council is to register medical practitioners. Its Fitness to Practice Committee hears complaints against doctors. Irish doctors, along with their British counterparts, had originally been registered under the Medical Act of 1858. In 1927 the Medical Registration Council was established along with a separate register for Irish doctors. Both the 1927 Act and the Medical Registration Council continued until the Medical Council was formed. The Medical Practitioners Bill which strengthened the role of laypersons on the Medical Council was passed by the Dáil in the first half of 2007.

As the period ended, the Department of Health and Children and the Health Service Executive were seeking to negotiate a new contract with consultants. This would see the consultants' working week extended to 39 hours and would reduce or eliminate their off-site private practice. Consultants would be available to work on a shift basis so that patients would be more likely to be seen by a consultant than by a junior doctor.[20] In other words, medical services in hospitals would be provided by consultants rather than led by consultants.

NURSES
Origins

Several major strands can be identified in the development of nursing in Ireland. As the report of the Commission on Nursing (1998) put it:[21]

> Three major influences shaped the development of nursing as a profession in Ireland—the religious orders of nursing sisters, scientific progress in the prevention and treatment of illness and disease, and the life and writings of Florence Nightingale.

In the 19th century, religious orders of nuns established hospitals to provide for the sick poor. While the workhouses and the infirmaries attached to them, set up by local authorities, were harsh institutions designed to discourage persons from using them, the sisters saw the nursing of the poor as a vocation. Their hospitals, which included St Vincent's in Dublin, the Mater in Dublin and Belfast and the Mercy in Cork, provided care of a high standard.

As knowledge of the connection between sanitary conditions and infection grew, the maintenance of hygiene in the hospital became a major concern of the nursing profession.

This was underlined by the work of Florence Nightingale who, through her Nightingale School opened at St Thomas' Hospital in London in 1860, influenced the development of nursing as a profession involving high standards of training and high personal standards for its nurses. It is interesting to note that Florence Nightingale applied to be accepted as a trainee at St Vincent's Hospital in Dublin but was turned down, apparently because she was not a sister.

The religious orders saw nursing as a profession for its sisters. Florence Nightingale, as the Commission report points out, paralleled this by 'promoting nursing as a profession for laywomen.'

Her insistence that trainee nurses come from 'respectable' families and be above reproach was no less than that of the nuns. She also expected these trainees to take posts of responsibility in the hospitals in which they worked and to pass on their standards to new student nurses. Many Irish matrons were trained according to Florence Nightingale's principles and did, indeed, pass them on.

Gradually, the voluntary hospitals opened their own training schools. A Dublin Metropolitan School of Nursing was opened in the 1890s thanks largely to Margaret Huxley, matron of Sir Patrick Duns Hospital. Huxley came to have an international reputation for her work in educating nurses.

The training of nurses was through an apprenticeship system in which the young nurses learned from senior nurses and in which it was the young trainee nurses who formed the bulk of the workforce.

The report of the Commission on Nursing put it as follows:

Young women entering the world of nursing found themselves in a strictly disciplined, regimented environment where good behaviour, obedience and dedication to their vocation were absolute requirements. Many of them were working in religious-controlled hospitals where the regimen and restrictions imposed by their superiors bore comparison with that of a religious community. But, if the disciplines imposed by the nursing management of the religious hospitals were strict, so too were those of the boards and matrons of the lay hospitals.

Whatever one may think today of the insistence by Florence Nightingale and by the nuns that student nurses be from 'respectable' families, it has to be conceded that they managed to make nursing an acceptable and even attractive employment to the middle and upper classes. As the Commission report puts it:

> Many occupations were seen as having unacceptable working-class connotations that breached the usually recognised dividing lines between the social classes, but following the reform of the profession, a career in nursing became acceptable ... It combined a caring activity with a career; with the further attraction that its training and experience could be a beneficial preparation for marriage. Remuneration was a secondary consideration.

The same standards did not apply in the area of psychiatric nursing. Generally speaking, the religious orders did not involve themselves in psychiatric hospitals at the time and this no doubt contributed to poorer standards in those institutions than in hospitals run by nuns. Rather than nurses, these hospitals had attendants. Men were looked after by male attendants and women by female attendants. Until the 1930s, there was little encouragement for psychiatric nurses or attendants to become trained.

Midwifery developed somewhat separately to general nursing. Generally speaking, women gave birth in their own homes into the early decades of this century and a so-called 'handywoman' would be called on if help was needed. The 'handywoman' was a sort of traditional, untrained midwife. It was not until the dispensaries were opened in 1851 that trained midwives began to be appointed and by 1905 there were 605 of them. However, they faced an uphill battle in convincing local people of their usefulness and their pay was so poor that many relied on their families to sustain them.[22] Local people continued to turn to the handywoman, sometimes with fatal consequences due to septicaemia arising from the handywoman's ignorance of sources of infection.

As mentioned elsewhere,[23] public health nursing was provided largely on a voluntary basis by nurses employed by Queen Victoria's Jubilee Institute for Nurses established in 1890. The Institute provided district nurses in many rural areas. The Lady Dudley Nursing Scheme, which began in 1903, provided a similar service in the West and in the Northwest. The appointment of midwives to the dispensaries can be seen as the beginnings of the development of a district nursing service paid for out of taxation.

The Irish Matrons Association was founded in 1904. Its leading lights were Margaret Huxley and Alice Reeves and both became major figures in the development of nurse training in Ireland and in the campaign to have the profession of nursing regulated. The Irish Matrons Association had as one of its main aims the promotion of the education of nurses. It originated in a group of nurses who had come together to raise money for an address of welcome to Queen Victoria on her visit to Ireland in 1900. They wished to recognise her establishment of the Queen Victoria's Jubilee Institute for Nurses. Having come together for this purpose, they then went on to form a Nurses Club. They then formed the Irish Nurses Association in 1900 so that nurses could discuss matters of mutual interest. The Irish Matrons Association followed and both organisations were closely linked, often having the same officers.[24] The Irish Matrons Association is now the Irish Association of Directors of Nursing and Midwifery.

1919 to 1990

Midwifery began to be regulated through the Midwives (Ireland) Act, 1918. The regulation of midwifery was conducted by the Central Midwives Board but the Commission's report notes that the handywomen continued in business until the 1930s.

General nursing was first regulated by the Nurses Registration (Ireland) Act, 1919, which established a General Nursing Council for Ireland. This system was separate to the system for midwifery. The Commission report notes that while legislation covering the medical profession permitted self-regulation, that governing nursing and midwifery placed the emphasis on control and supervision.

The Central Midwives Board was replaced by An Bord Altranais (The Nursing Board) in 1951 when the 1919 Act was updated by the Nurses Act, 1950. An Bord Altranais, which replaced the General Nursing Council also, registers nurses and regulates the education of nurses. A majority of its members are themselves nurses and a majority of these nurses are elected by the nurses on the register. A Fitness to Practice Committee was appointed by An Bord Altranais following the recommendations of a working party set up by the Minister for Health in 1975.

Traditionally, the working conditions of nurses were poor. As has been mentioned earlier, nurses worked in a very regimented setting with demanding expectations concerning their behaviour. They were expected to see themselves as persons with a vocation, and with very good marriage prospects who should not concern themselves overly with the issue of pay. Not only was their pay low but most nurses were not pensionable as the Hospitals Commission noted in 1945.

Organisation in an industrial relations sense began with the formation of the Irish Asylum Workers Union in 1917 which engaged in disputes on behalf of its members. In 1919, the Irish Nurses Union was formed as part of the Irish Women Workers Union. The Irish Nurses Organisation evolved from the Irish Nurses Union in 1949.

It had limited registration as a trade union and obtained full registration in 1988. Nurses are also organised by SIPTU, IMPACT and the Psychiatric Nurses Association. However, the INO remains the biggest union for nurses in Ireland.

The first Nursing Adviser was appointed to the Department of Health in 1949. The development of community and public health nursing was provided for in the Health Acts of 1947 and 1953. The term 'public health nurse' was introduced by the Minister for Health in 1958 to replace the term 'district nurse'.

The replacement of attendants by fully trained psychiatric nurses was not completed in the psychiatric hospitals until the 1960s. From 1919, persons certified by the Royal Medico-Psychological Association were accepted for registration by the General Nursing Council of Ireland. However, from 1935 persons wishing to be registered as psychiatric nurses were required to pass the Council's own examinations. Courses leading to recognition for mental handicap nurses were initiated in 1959.

1990 to 2006

The education of nurses began to change significantly in 1994 when Galway University Hospital School of Nursing introduced a diploma course for student nurses. This was followed by other diploma courses in other universities and today nurses qualify through a degree course involving both practical and academic work. Nurse training became a degree course from the 2002–2003 academic year, thus bringing an end to the old apprenticeship system.

The Commission on Nursing was established in 1997 as one of a package of measures to avert a strike. In effect, the work of the Commission led, and continues to lead, to a modernising of the profession of nursing both in terms of management and of clinical practice. It enhanced the status of nursing and led to the provision of promotional opportunity for nurses which recognised their clinical expertise.

Despite the issuing of the report, a nurses' strike took place in 1999. The strike gave impetus to the implementation of the report but, perhaps more importantly, it underlined that nurses were now prepared to take action in their own interest.

Thereafter nurses, particularly in the Irish Nurses Organisation, campaigned vocally over conditions for patients in A&E departments, in nursing homes and in other areas in which they worked.

Shortages of nurses occurred both in the mid-1970s and in the years following the beginning of the economic boom of the mid-90s and onwards. As a consequence, beds were closed because they could not be staffed and surgical procedures were cancelled either because of an absence of theatre nurses, of nurses to staff surgical beds or of intensive care nurses. Irish hospitals sent their directors of nursing to South Africa, India, the Philippines and other countries to recruit nurses to make up the deficit. By 2005, problems arising from nurse shortages had eased considerably although not entirely.

In more recent years, the specialist nurse has become a more common phenomenon. As McCarthy (1997) notes, specialist nurses such as diabetic nurse specialists and critical care nurses were increasingly appearing in clinics in the 1990s.[25] Reflecting the ageing of the population, nurses specialising in 'maintaining maximum levels of independence, physical and cognitive functioning' among patients in long-stay hospitals have emerged.

In a further development in the clinical scope of nurses, the Irish Medicines Board (Miscellaneous Provisions) Act, 2006, provides for authority to be given to nurses to prescribe certain medicines.

The National Council for the Professional Development of Nursing and Midwifery was established in 1999 in the light of recommendations of the Commission on Nursing report. Its functions include monitoring the ongoing development of nursing and midwifery specialities; supporting additional developments in nurse education; and determining the appropriate level of qualification and experience for entry into specialist nursing and midwifery practice.[26]

CONCLUSION
As the period ends, the medical and nursing professions stand on the brink of change. General practice appears to be about to undergo major development while the environment for

consultants is changing with a desire by the Department of Health and Children and the Health Service Executive to move to a consultant-provided rather than a consultant-led public hospital service and with an increasing number of private hospitals promised. Nurses are increasingly specialising and are about to acquire authorisation to prescribe; and it seems likely that the recent move to a degree course as the basic form of nurse education and training will bring profound change to the profession.

Chapter 8 ∽

FINANCING THE HEALTH SYSTEM

INTRODUCTION

The health services were funded mainly or partly by local ratepayers until 1977. In the middle decades of the 20th century, the Irish Hospitals Sweepstakes paid for the building of many hospitals. By the end of the period, the financing of public health services had moved fully from local taxation to central government. In addition, substantial sums of money were paid for private health services through the VHI and other insurers. The end of the period saw a growing concern with costs and with the question of whether funds raised for the health services were being spent effectively.

Origins

From the late 19th century and until 1947, the cost of the public health services was borne almost entirely by local authorities which derived their funding from local ratepayers. Some assistance from central government was provided with the introduction of grants, namely the Estate Duty Grant introduced in 1888 and the Licence Duty Grant introduced in 1898 (Hensey, 1979).[1]

The Licence Duty Grant, for example, made a contribution towards the salaries of doctors in workhouses and dispensaries, nurses in workhouses, officers of the sanitary authorities and towards the cost of medicines and medical appliances.

The absence of central funding held back the pace of development of health services. Voluntary hospitals funded out of philanthropic donations were set up mainly in Dublin in the 19th century. Outside Dublin, a system of general hospitals developed only very slowly and in conjunction with the workhouses.

For most of the first half of the 20th century, the main burden of financing the health services continued to fall on the rates. Some grants were made by central government to part-finance the cost of special services. These included the tuberculosis service, the school medical service, maternity and child welfare schemes and venereal diseases schemes. In the 1930s, state grants to provide free milk for poorer children were introduced.

The Hospitals Trust Fund provided a substantial boost to the development of hospitals. The Fund was financed by sweepstakes on horse races. The initiative to fund hospitals in this way had come from the voluntary hospitals around 1930. However, the sweepstakes became a major source of capital funding for public hospitals under the Public Hospitals Act, 1933. The sweepstakes also contributed to capital and revenue costs in voluntary hospitals.

Health services also benefited, to a degree, from the National Insurance Scheme. The scheme made cash payments to workers who were prevented from earning because of ill health. When the funds in the scheme exceeded what was needed for that purpose, the extra funds were used to subsidise the cost to members of hospital treatment and of dental and optical treatment. The amount spent under the scheme depended entirely on the amount of the surplus. As soon as the surplus was spent in any one year, these additional health benefits were dropped.

A proposal to fund the entire health service through insurance contributions was made in 1944 by the Bishop of Clonfert, Dr Duignan. Dr Duignan suggested that the National Insurance

Scheme should manage the scheme. The monies raised, he believed, could be used to develop the service. His proposal was turned down by the State. At about the same time, the Irish Medical Association published proposals for a health insurance scheme for the middle classes. This also was not taken up at the time.[2]

However, central government was now ready to play a significant role in paying for health services. Hensey (1979) notes that in 1947 State grants met only 16% of the cost of providing health services. The remainder was raised by ratepayers. But the situation improved from the viewpoint of the local authorities following the passing of the Health Services (Financial Provisions) Act, 1947. Under the Act, the maximum contribution by the local authorities would be the equivalent of their contribution in the year ending March 1948, plus half of any amount over that. The remainder would be paid by the Exchequer. The scheme was meant to relieve the burden on local ratepayers so as to remove any reluctance on their part to expand the health services locally. But thanks to inflation and to the increasing development of health services, the burden remained substantial.

Overall spending on health services was low, seen from today's perspective. In 1957 the proportion of Gross National Product spent on health services was 2.87%.[3]

Part-financing of the health services out of local taxation ended in 1977. This change had been proposed in the 1966 White Paper, *The Health Services and their Further Development*.[4] The White Paper had pointed out that a majority of acute hospital in-patients were now being treated in teaching and regional hospitals which transcended county boundaries (Boland, 1997).[5]

Other reasons given for the transfer of funding to central government were:

- The health system needed to be expanded and this would mean substantial extra costs which could not be met out of local rates.

- The amount of rates which could be raised by various local authorities varied from one to another and some were, as a result, at a disadvantage in their capacity to pay for health services (Wiley, 1997).[6]

THE HOSPITALS TRUST FUND

The Hospitals Trust Fund was the main source of finance for the building and equipping of hospitals in the 1940s and 1950s (Hensey, 1979) and it continued raising money until the 1980s. The Fund originated in a sweepstake organised by voluntary hospitals in 1930. The venture was so successful that the government took control of the enterprise under the Public Hospitals Act, 1933.

The Fund raised money from the sale of sweepstake tickets for horse races. The tickets were sold in Ireland and around the world, especially in the United States. The decision on where the money would be spent was made by the Minister for Health of the day on the advice of the Hospitals Commission which had been set up for that purpose.

The Fund financed, almost fully, the public hospital building programme. It thus made a major contribution towards the provision and expansion of public hospitals around the country. It made grants towards the revenue of voluntary hospitals. The latter also received capitation grants from the Department of Health until 1974.

Fees from patients and fundraising had been the main sources of money for the voluntary hospitals. In six hospitals, before World War One, the income from paying patients averaged £2,000 a year. In the 1920s two Dublin hospitals began to run a sweepstake on major horse races. Though these were illegal, Taylor (1997) says that the government turned a blind eye to them.[7]

Taylor describes the evolution of the Irish Hospitals Sweepstakes as follows:

Eventually the Public Charitable Hospitals Temporary Provision Act of 1930 under which the Irish Hospitals Sweepstakes started [stipulated that] 25% of the beds in the voluntary hospitals must be made available for patients who were unable to pay, or where the charge was not more than 10 shillings per week. In 1930 the first official sweepstakes were held on the Manchester November Handicap and the first three sweepstakes made £1.25 million. The first sweepstake was shared by six hospitals, the second was shared by twenty and the third by 40 hospitals.

The government then introduced an amendment to the Act in 1931 ensuring that two thirds of the income went to voluntary hospitals and one third to local authority hospitals. In 1933 the Public Hospitals Act gave legal authority to set up the Hospitals Commission which was to survey hospital facilities.

The Sweep of 1931 was on the English Derby from which St Vincent's received £21,000. Up to 1969 St Vincent's Hospital, St Stephen's Green, received £2,100,000 and St Vincent's at Elm Park received over £3 million.

The Irish Hospitals Sweepstakes was the brainchild of Richard Duggan, a bookmaker, Joe McGrath, a former minister in the Free State government, and Spencer Freeman, an engineer.

In the 1930s, Ireland became internationally known for its sweepstakes and received world press coverage. It was declared illegal in the United States and Great Britain though the majority of tickets continued to be sold there. It was a huge source of employment for women at their headquarters in Ballsbridge where the draws took place three or four times a year.[8]

The Sweepstakes continued until the early 1980s, by which time their contribution to overall health costs had lost significance.

THE EVOLUTION OF HEALTH SPENDING SINCE THE 1980s

By the end of the period covered by this book, almost the entire cost of the public health services was being met by the Exchequer. Curry (2003) notes that Health Contributions and hospital outpatient charges made up just over 10% of the cost.[9]

The 1980s was a period of cutbacks and spending restraints in the health services due to concern over the national debt. The cuts were profound. Spending on health which had stood at 7.72% of Gross Domestic Product in 1980 had been pared back to 7.04% by 1985. Deep cuts imposed by the Fianna Fáil government elected in 1987 reduced the proportion again to 5.72% in 1990.

At the time of writing, the economy is buoyant and it is important to understand the context in which the health cuts of the 1980s and early 1990s took place. This context is succinctly explained in the Deloitte & Touche report, *Value for Money Audit of the Irish Health System* (2001) as follows:[10]

Irish governments during the 1980s were faced with a series of difficult economic conditions. Unemployment levels were consistently high throughout the decade peaking at 17% of the labour force in 1987. The National Debt to GNP ratio reached 131% during the period and governments were forced to borrow to meet day-to-day current expenditure. GNP growth averaged a minimal 0.2% per annum during the period 1980 to 1986.

In the late 1980s governments adopted policies of fiscal rectitude and made significant cuts in public expenditure to restore order to the public finances. From 1986 to 1989, current expenditure fell by 10% of GNP. The reductions in public expenditure had the effect of reducing the Exchequer Borrowing Requirement towards the end of the decade and creating an environment of modest economic growth in the period 1987 to 1989.

The health sector, as a large public spending department, was one of the hardest affected by the severe cutbacks in

expenditure during this decade. By 1986, it is estimated that
health spending was some 8.5% lower than in 1981 taking into
account inflation, the impact of demographic change and
advances in medical technology. Net non-capital public expenditure on health in the 1986 to 1989 period remained virtually
static at c.£1.2bn per annum.

The effect of the cuts in spending was to reduce bed numbers to
very low levels by European standards.

Significant rationalisation of the Irish hospital system also took
place at this time, with the closure of a number of voluntary and
Health Board-controlled hospitals. The most significant impact of
these closures can be seen in the reduction in bed capacity in the
Irish healthcare system in the period 1983 to 1990. During this
decade, acute in-patient bed numbers in public hospitals dropped
from some 15,163 at the end of 1983 to 11,766 by the end of 1989, a
reduction of 3,397 beds or 22%; this number remained virtually
unchanged throughout the whole of the 1990s. Approximately
2,000 of the reduction in bed numbers occurred in the Eastern
region, representing 29% of the beds in the region. The biggest
part of this reduction occurred between 1986 and 1988 at the time
of the stringent budgetary cutbacks, when 2,200 beds were taken
out of the system in a short period. These bed reductions took
place against a background of Ireland having an already low ratio
of beds per 1,000 population. By 1990, Ireland had an average of
3.9 in-patient beds per 1,000 population, less than half the EU
average at that time of 8.2. Within the EU, only the UK had a lower
ratio at 2.3 per 1,000 population in 1990. Significant reductions in
numbers employed in the system arose in the latter part of the
1980s—57,275 people were employed in the health service in 1989
compared to 64,889 eight years earlier.

Economic growth in the mid-1990s brought increased health
spending which had risen to 7.39% of GDP by 2002. Most of the

extra money was spent on pay for new and existing staff (Curry, 2003).

Despite the continuing espousal of community care by governments,[11] the lion's share of the revenue allocation for health services went to general hospitals. By the end of the period they were receiving about half of all expenditure while community care received between a quarter and one third of expenditure.

HEALTH CONTRIBUTIONS

As mentioned earlier, a proportion of the cost of running the health services was met by local rates until 1977. By the mid-1960s, it had become clear that this was no longer an appropriate source of funding for an expanding health service. Therefore, this cost had been transferred to the central Exchequer by 1977. Meanwhile, a new source of funds had been created by the Health Contributions Act, 1971. Under the Act, taxpayers made a contribution towards the cost of the health services based on their income up to a certain limit. Since 1991, the earnings limit has been removed and the contribution has been 2% of earnings.

COMMISSION ON HEALTH FUNDING

The issue of the funding of hospital services and of access to these services have been interlinked in public debate for some decades. In the 1990s, Curry (2003) notes, waiting lists became the norm for public patients. Membership of the VHI grew as persons sought the faster access to hospital care which private insurance provided.

Since much private care was delivered in public and voluntary hospitals in which 20% of the beds were designated for private patients, the issue of access to these beds was raised.

The Commission on Health Funding, which reported in 1989, recommended that a system made up of both public and private healthcare should continue.[12] However, it sought the introduction of a common waiting list so that there would be no distinction between public and private patients in relation to access to a hospital bed.

The state system should not subsidise private care given that it was already providing a service for the population. Tax relief on VHI contributions, it recommended, should be dropped.

Against this view it has been argued that the use by private patients of public facilities at less than the full economic cost is justified by the fact that these private patients through their taxes are already paying for the public facilities they use.

The White Paper, *Private Health Insurance* (1999)[13] states that:

> . . . a case can be made in favour of some level of State incentive to the individual to effect private health insurance, on the basis that those who opt for private cover effectively forgo a statutory entitlement while continuing to contribute to the funding of the public health service through taxation.

It adds, however, that:

> . . . there is a need to address issues relating to the pricing of public hospital beds at less than the full economic cost. In developing new charging arrangements for public hospital services to private patients, the extent and pace of adjustment, while allowing for medical inflation, will be sensitive to the need for continuing stability in the private health insurance market.

The Commission on Health Funding, as Curry (2003) notes, had been established in 1987 at a time of cutbacks in health spending and of considerable controversy over these cutbacks.

However, the Commission concluded that the difficulties in the health services owed more to the way these services were organised than to funding.[14]

It summed up its position as follows:

The kernel of the Commission's conclusions is that the solution to the problem facing the Irish health services does not lie primarily in the system of funding but rather in the way that services are planned, organised and delivered.

Referring to the delivery of health services it stated that:

The rationing system in place in acute hospitals is based to some extent on ability to pay and, indeed, to some extent on arbitrary criteria, such as accidents of geography or timing, or indeed even personal persistence. It is inequitable that patients in medically similar circumstances do not have equal access to services. As a result, unnecessary frustration and suffering is caused to those on long waiting lists.

In considering how health services should be financed, the Commission concluded that the Exchequer should continue to be the main source of funding. This arrangement would enable the government to make and implement health policy, to regulate access and also to ensure fairness in how people paid for services.

Private insurance as the main source of funding, on the other hand, could deprive high-risk groups of a service, could be difficult to enforce and would not offer any advantages over the public model in terms of controlling costs.

Compulsory health insurance for all, one of the options it had considered, was simply another form of taxation, a majority of the Commission members believed. It recommended the abolition of the Health Contribution.

It criticised the direct funding by the Department of Health of the voluntary hospitals. This relationship meant that the voluntary hospitals did not report to the health boards which were running the public hospitals. It also meant that the Department of Health was concerned with managing services whereas the Commission believed that the proper role of the department and the Minister was to make health policy.

The Commission suggested that a new authority be set up to manage health services.

Some of the Commission's recommendations were later reflected in changes in the organisation of health services. The Health (Amendment) (No. 3) Act, 1996, laid the groundwork for separating the policy functions of the Department of Health from the operational functions of other agencies.

Funding of voluntary public hospitals by the health boards, rather than the Department of Health, began in 1998.

Citing the Commission's report, the Minister for Health, Dr Rory O'Hanlon TD, announced in 1991 that a new health authority for the greater Dublin area would be set up to replace the Eastern Health Board. The Eastern Regional Health Authority was established under legislation passed in 1999. The ERHA was operational from 1 March 2000. It took over the funding of voluntary hospitals and of the main agencies for intellectually disabled people from the Department of Health. The Eastern Health Board was replaced by three area health boards. These were the East Coast Area Health Board, the Northern Area Health Board and the South Western Area Health Board.

The common waiting list recommended by the Commission was not introduced, though the 2001 health strategy[15] adopted new measures to improve access by public patients to hospital beds. Neither was the Health Contribution abolished.

Tax relief on private health insurance was not abolished, as sought by the Commission, but was reduced from the marginal (highest) rate to the standard rate. The change was phased in over two years, 1995/96 and 1996/97.

With questions of funding and of access to health services continuing to loom large in public debate, an audit of the value for money provided by the health service was commissioned by the Department of Health and Children from Deloitte & Touche, management consultants.

In their report, they pointed to problems which arose from the underfunding of services in the 1980s.[16] They saw the growing demand for healthcare and the growing cost of that care as the fundamental problem facing the health services. As the report put it:

> The fundamental problem facing the health services in Ireland and elsewhere is the growth in demand and healthcare costs. The demand is driven by a range of factors including public expectations, demographics, the availability of new diagnostic and therapeutic approaches to care, and significant techno-logical developments in medicine, including drugs.

The 2001 health strategy again addressed the issue of access. Access would be improved, it suggested, by a number of measures:

- 3,000 of the beds lost to the system because of the health cuts of the late 1980s and early 1990s would be restored over a 10-year period to the end of 2011. These beds would be exclusively for public patients.
- More hospital consultants would be employed.
- Any adult waiting longer than three months for hospital treatment would be provided with private treatment in Ireland or elsewhere by the National Treatment Purchase Fund which would be established for that purpose.[17]

THE NATIONAL TREATMENT PURCHASE FUND
The establishment of the National Treatment Purchase Fund formed part of the *Health Strategy, 2001*.

It was seen as a mechanism to allow two objectives in the Health Strategy to be met: that no adult would wait longer than six months and no child longer than three months to begin treatment following referral from a consultant; and that by the end of 2004, no public patient would wait longer than three months.

The NTPF arranges treatment, free of charge, for those public patients who have been longest on the waiting list. Treatment is provided in private hospitals in Ireland and the UK.

The first treatments under the NTPF were carried out in 2002. By April 2006, a total of 42,000 people had been treated.

In 2004, the NTPF was also assigned the role of compiling hospital waiting lists because of inaccuracies in the traditional waiting lists. The latter had, on analysis by the NTPF, been found to include people who no longer required treatment, who were no longer available for treatment, who were not medically suitable for treatment or who had asked to postpone treatment.[18]

By April 2006, the Patient Treatment Register covered nineteen hospitals and 74% of historical waiting list data. The register showed that, almost five years after the publication of the *Health Strategy, 2001,*

- 41% of patients were waiting 3–6 months for a surgical procedure.
- 35% of patients were waiting 6–12 months for a surgical procedure.
- 24% of patients were waiting over 12 months for a surgical procedure.
- 85% of the most common adult surgical procedures were waiting less than 6 months.
- 87% of the most common child surgical procedures were waiting less than 6 months.[19]

CASEMIX

The Commission on Health Funding recommended that hospitals should be funded on the basis of agreed levels of service. These levels, in turn, should be based on the types of treatment actually provided to patients rather than based, for instance, on historical budgets. This is known as the 'casemix system'.

The Department of Health responded by establishing the National Casemix Project in 1991.

The casemix approach was gradually implemented from 1993. Modernisation of the National Casemix Programme was announced by the Minister for Health and Children, Micheál Martin TD, in 2004.[20]

The casemix system has built-in incentive for hospitals, the Minister explained:

> Ireland operates a unique 'budget-neutral' Casemix policy—any funding saved through efficiencies is reinvested with hospitals who have demonstrated that additional funding allocated to them will result in real benefits. Casemix is not used to reduce acute hospital funding.[21]

PRIVATE FUNDING

Wiley (1997) notes that the public component of health expenditure fell from 85% in the 1980s to 75% in the mid-1990s. The other 25%, she states, is accounted for by the private sector. This is made up of health insurance companies, general practitioners, pharmacists and private hospitals.[22]

This proportion has remained constant. For instance, it was estimated that in 2001, 24% of health expenditure was from private sources (Purcell, 2003).[23]

According to the White Paper, *Private Health Insurance* (1999):

> Out of a total national health expenditure in excess of £4 billion (€5 billion), private health insurance contributes approximately £350 million (€444 million)—most of which relates to hospital services—with about £85 million (€108 million) going directly to the public hospital system.

ELIGIBILITY FOR HOSPITAL SERVICES

In 1957, when the VHI was established, entitlement to hospital services was income-based in a three-tier system. Those on the lowest incomes were entitled to free hospital treatment, those on the highest incomes (about 15% of the population) had no entitlement and the middle group had some entitlement to free or subsidised treatment.

The Health Act, 1970, continued the three-tier system. The middle income group was now described as having 'limited eligibility' for hospital services. But when the Health Contributions mentioned above were introduced under the Health Contributions Act, 1971, hospital charges for persons with limited eligibility were abolished.

In 1974, the Minister for Health and Social Welfare, Brendan Corish TD, announced that entitlement to hospital services would be extended to everybody. Mr Corish's plan was stymied by hospital consultants who opposed the move on the basis that it would adversely affect their conditions of employment and their remuneration (Curry, 2003).

In 1979, his successor Charles Haughey TD extended the right to free hospital maintenance and treatment to all except a group made up of persons whose income exceeded £5,500 per annum and of farmers with valuations in excess of £60. The latter groups were entitled to free hospital services provided in the public wards but they remained liable for consultants' fees.

What this meant was that a three-tier eligibility system remained. In the first category were those who were entitled to a free GP service and free prescribed medicines as well as free hospital treatment as medical card holders. In the second category where those who were entitled to a free hospital service. And in the third category were those who were obliged to pay both for GP treatment and for specialist services provided by hospital consultants (Curry, 2003).

In 1991, the entitlement to free maintenance and treatment in a public ward was extended to all, regardless of income.

CONCLUSION

The past 50 years have seen virtually all public health spending transferred to central government. Though spending was cut in the late 1980s and early 1990s it is now at the highest level in the country's history.

Eligibility for free hospital services is at its broadest ever level with all citizens, regardless of income, entitled to a free service.

Nevertheless, private spending on health accounts for about 25% of the total, mainly in the form of the purchase of private health insurance and fees to GPs and specialists, the latter for outpatient consultations.

While debate continues about the relationship between private and public healthcare, it seems likely that both will continue to be a feature of the health system in the future.

Chapter 9 ◔

CONTROVERSY AND SCANDAL

INTRODUCTION

While we might prefer to see health services planned and implemented in a calm and reasoned way, the history of controversy and of scandal in the health system demonstrates that this is not always the case.

Clashes of ideology, self-interest and individual and systemic failings all play their part in how the health services work—or fail to work—and in how they are shaped.

Many controversies—such as the Mother and Child Scheme or the question of access to contraception—involved intense and heated debate in their day but were neutral in their effect on perceptions of the health system. It could be argued that it was the Catholic Church, and not the health system, which suffered the greatest loss of public esteem in these controversies.

In recent decades, however, it is scandals in the health system that have most affected public perceptions. Revelations concerning practices that led to loss of life, permanent injury or illness have ended the era of unquestioning acceptance of the views of doctors or of bodies administering health services.

This chapter looks at some of the more significant of these controversies and scandals.

ORIGINS

The Catholic Church's suspicion of the intentions of the State laid the groundwork for one of the great controversies of the 20th century, the Mother and Child Scheme.

As Mahon (1997) points out, the Catholic Church was deeply opposed to excessive control by the State which it likened to communism.[1] This opposition was underpinned by a papal encyclical, *Quadragesimo Anno* (1931).

Proposals by the State to extend health and social services could be seen as attempts to undermine the family. Ferriter (2004) notes that there were even Catholic doctors who saw the immunisation of children against deadly infections as an infringement of the rights of the family.[2]

MOTHER AND CHILD SCHEME

Reference has been made a number of times in this history to the controversy generated by the so-called Mother and Child Scheme. This is because the controversy and its outcome were of fundamental importance to the relationship between government and the Church concerning the health services. The controversy also involved what might be called the full-blooded participation of the Irish Medical Association on the same side as the Church. While the IMA emerged more or less unscathed, the Church suffered long-term damage to its standing in the eyes of the people.

The Scheme had its origins in the Public Health Bill, 1945. The Bill proposed to allow local health authorities to provide a free health service to children up to the age of sixteen years. It would also give the health authorities the power to have schoolchildren medically inspected and to educate mothers and children on health issues.

The Church opposed the concept of compulsory medical inspection. Such a measure would breach the rights of parents, it argued, and it also considered it undesirable that adolescent girls should be medically inspected (Mahon, 1997).

The Irish Medical Association also opposed the Bill. Mahon suggests that the Association was motivated by the fear that free antenatal and maternity services would affect the income of doctors. Mahon outlines the objections by the IMA as follows:

- Payment of the doctor as an independent contractor by the family underpinned the relationship between the two.
- Parents had a duty to provide for the health of their children and a free medical service would undermine this role.
- The State was not entitled to take on a health education role. Doctors and the church were the ones who should provide such education.[3]

Barrington suggests the Church was fearful that the Bill would pave the way for information on sex education to be given to children and for women to be given information about contraception or even about abortion.[4]

The Fianna Fáil government which had produced the Bill was defeated in a general election in 1948. A coalition government took power and Noel Browne TD was appointed Minister for Health. The Bill had been superseded by the Health Bill, 1947, which became the Health Act, 1947, but controversy continued.

The Church and the medical profession continued their opposition. Noel Browne showed little subtlety in dealing with the issue and managed to worsen relationships with the doctors and the bishops. Browne resigned and in the 1951 general election health was a major issue. Fianna Fáil returned to power. It reintroduced the Mother and Child Scheme but without the provisions for the education of women by health authorities and without compulsory medical examination of children. Moreover, the free medical service for children would be provided until the child was six, not sixteen.

Both the doctors and the bishops had won a victory of sorts. But for the bishops it was a Pyrrhic victory. As Barrington notes, the bishops were seen by the public as having gone too far. Government departments and ministers gradually became less responsive to representations from individual bishops. Moreover the Mother and Child Scheme was raised in criticisms of Church interference well into the 1970s in public debate, as the author recalls.

For the doctors, though, it was by no means a Pyrrhic victory. The Church took the blame and paid the price. The role of the Irish Medical Association was little mentioned in subsequent debate.

CONTRACEPTION

While access to 'artificial' means of contraception was a major political and health issue in the 1970s, it had been very much in the minds of Catholic bishops and clergy for many decades before that. As mentioned elsewhere, the fear that women would be told about contraception had been a factor in the bishops' opposition to the Public Health Bill, 1945.

The Church's opposition to contraception, divorce and abortion had deep roots. In modern times it can be traced back to a 1930 encyclical, *Casti Connubii*, which made the family the basis of morality and social order. It was in response to Church lobbying arising out of the ideas expressed in this encyclical that the Censorship of Publications Act, 1929, banned the publication of information on contraception and abortion. In 1935, the Criminal Law (Amendment) Act banned the importation and sale of contraceptives. And the 1937 Constitution reflected Catholic social teaching (Mahon, 1997).

But the Church was not concerned only with artificial contraception. It also worried about the use of the so-called 'safe period'. Farmar (1994) quotes a Canon McCarthy who, in the 1940s, suggested that if knowledge of the safe period became widespread, then the safe period might be used 'indiscriminately' and that this would be a 'situation fraught with calamitous circumstances'.[5] The use of the safe period by married couples in limited circumstances[6] was justified by Pope Pius XII[7] in 1951. In 1963, Holles Street Hospital opened a 'marriage guidance' clinic, the purpose of which was to advise mothers about the safe period. Even that modest move was resisted by some nurses and obstetricians (Farmar, 1994).

The Church repeated its opposition to artificial contraception in the 1968 encyclical, *Humanae Vitae*. However, in 1969 a fertility guidance clinic was opened in Dublin with the support of the Family Planning Rights Group and of the International Planned Parenthood Association. The clinic got around the law prohibiting the sale of contraceptives by giving them away for free, with clients invited to make donations. Clinics were also set up in some other towns and cities.

Nevertheless, contraceptives remained inaccessible to most people except where GPs were prepared to prescribe the contraceptive pill as a cycle regulator. The major change in the situation came in 1973 when the Supreme Court in *McGee vs Attorney General* found that married couples were entitled to obtain contraceptives for their personal use. This finding rendered unconstitutional Section 17 of the 1935 Act.

The Health (Family Planning) Act, 1979, introduced by the Minister for Health, Charles Haughey TD, allowed GPs to prescribe contraceptives for medical reasons or for *bona fide* family planning purposes. As a compromise it did not please those who supported the wide availability of contraception because of the requirement to get a prescription in order to get a contraceptive. Haughey himself called it 'an Irish solution to an Irish problem'.

The restrictions introduced by the 1979 Act were removed in 1985 when the coalition government introduced amendments allowing condoms to be sold freely to persons aged eighteen or more. In 1993 the Health (Family Planning) Amendment Act placed an obligation on health boards to provide family planning services.

St Ita's Hospital, Portrane, a leading example of an old-style psychiatric hospital, with its own extensive farm. (*Derek Speirs*)

The VHI management team 1957 to 1965. *Back row*: G.B. Savage, B.J. Payne. *Front row*: R.M. Graham, N.J. Burke, J.F. O'Mahony. (*Vhi Healthcare*)

Founded in 1861 by the Sisters of Mercy, the Mater Misericordiae in Eccles Street, Dublin, remains one of Ireland's leading medical centres. (*Courtesy of the National Library of Ireland*)

The demand for availability of artificial means of contraception was a major political and health issue in the 1970s and 1980s. (*Derek Speirs*)

Charles J. Haughey TD, Minister for Health and later Taoiseach, in 1979 extended the right to free hospital maintenance and treatment to all except those on the highest incomes, who remained liable for consultants' fees. (*Derek Speirs*)

From 2000, the BreastCheck programme offered free screening for breast cancer to women aged between 50 and 64, in some parts of the country, and was due to be extended nationwide. (*Photocall Ireland*)

Mr Tom Ryan, Chief Executive of the VHI from 1983 to 1994, was the first Irish Chairman of the International Federation of Health Plans. (*Vhi Healthcare*)

Mr Noel Fox (*standing, right*) who was appointed Recovery Manager of the VHI following a major financial deficit in 1988. (*Vhi Healthcare*)

Mr Noel Hanlon, Chairman of the VHI from 1992 to 1997. (*Vhi Healthcare*)

Dr Rory O'Hanlon TD, Minister for Health, ended the direct funding of voluntary hospitals by the Department of Health. (*Derek Speirs*)

Mr Derry Hussey, Chairman of Vhi Healthcare, 1997–2003, welcomed competition for Vhi Healthcare. (*Vhi Healthcare*)

Mr Vincent Sheridan became Chief Executive of Vhi Healthcare in 2001. (*Vhi Healthcare*)

From the 1980s, people with disabilities promoted a rights agenda. (*Derek Speirs*)

Rita Lawlor helped found the Dublin City Advocacy Group to promote the rights of persons with disabilities. Here she is seen talking to Mervyn Taylor, Minister for Equality and Law Reform in the 1990s. (*Derek Speirs*)

A task force established in 2002 under the chairmanship of Mr David Hanly recommended a major reorganisation of the hospital system, but the plan ran into local opposition. (*Photocall Ireland*)

The exposure of conditions at the Leas Cross nursing home in Dublin in 2005 raised concerns about the effectiveness of the system of regulation of nursing homes. (*Photocall Ireland*)

Mícheál Martin TD as Minister for Health introduced a ban on smoking in the workplace in 2004. (*Photocall Ireland*)

Mr Noel Burke, first General Manager of the VHI. (*Vhi Healthcare*)

Mr Desmond Cashell chaired the VHI through its recovery programme in the late 1980s and early 1990s. (*Vhi Healthcare*)

Mr Bernard Collins, who became Chairman of Vhi Healthcare in 2003, warned that delays in introducing risk equalisation threatened the future of the organisation. (*Vhi Healthcare*)

Mary Harney TD, Minister for Health and Children, commenced risk equalisation in January 2006. (*Derek Speirs*)

The increasing availability of contraceptives in the 1980s and 1990s helped to bring about a decline in the birth-rate (Mahon, 1997). The birth-rate had increased in the 1960s and 1970s but fell in the 1980s and 1990s. This is attributed by Mahon partly to younger women deferring their first pregnancy and partly to women having fewer children.

BLOOD PRODUCTS
The Blood Transfusion Service Board was involved in three scandals concerning blood and blood products, the aftermath of which continued into the early years of the new century.

Haemophiliacs
It emerged in the 1980s that a blood product called Factor VIII, imported by the BTSB from the United States and given to haemophiliacs, had infected more than half the 400 haemophiliacs in the Republic with HIV or Hepatitis C, and in some cases with both. Following a lengthy campaign by the Irish Haemophilia Society, the Lindsay Tribunal, chaired by Judge Alison Lindsay, was set up in 1999 to inquire into the matter. It reported in 2002. It found that there had been 'a failure to cease to use and to withdraw non-heated BTSB Factor IX in 1985 with due expedition.' It also criticised some doctors for using untreated blood products for too long.[8]

Anti-D
It emerged in the 1990s that more than 1,000 women had been infected with Hepatitis C by Anti-D immunoglobulin treatment using a blood product provided by the BTSB. A tribunal chaired by Mr Thomas Finlay, the former Chief Justice, was set up in 1996 to inquire into the matter. His report, published in 1997, was seriously critical of the BTSB.[9] Positive Action, a pressure group set up by infected women, campaigned on compensation and other issues.

Notification delay

It emerged during the course of the Finlay Tribunal that there had been a delay of, in some cases, months and in others of years in informing 28 blood donors that they had tested positive for Hepatitis C antibodies.

Following publication of the Lindsay Report, the Irish Blood Transfusion Service (successor to the BTSB) apologised publicly for 'all death and injury' caused by its products.

ORGAN RETENTION

Controversy over the retention of organs following post-mortems, especially of children, arose in 1999, following the exposure of similar practices in Britain. Parents of children whose organs had been 'harvested' without their knowledge or consent formed a pressure group called Parents for Justice. The Minister for Health and Children, Micheál Martin, set up an inquiry called the Dunne Inquiry in 2000. By 2005 the Inquiry had failed to publish a final report and it was brought to an end by the government. Dr Deirdre Madden, a law lecturer at University College Cork, was appointed to examine the documents that had been collected by the Dunne Inquiry and to produce a report.

Her report was published in 2006. Her principal findings were:

- Doctors believed at the time that they were sparing the feelings of parents by not telling them that their children's organs might be retained.
- This was the practice not only in Ireland but in other countries and, in fairness, doctors should be judged by the standards which prevailed at that time. That parents were not informed was 'not due to personal or individual misconduct, but rather to a system and culture that failed to take into account the views and feelings of parents.'

- However, expectations of transparency were growing in the 1990s and the medical profession, the Department of Health and hospitals should have realised this.
- More could have been done by the Department of Health and Children to reassure the public that although families were rightly concerned about the lack of consent for retention, the practices themselves were in line with best international standards.[10]

HYSTERECTOMIES—THE NEARY CASE

In 1990, two midwives at Our Lady of Lourdes Hospital in Drogheda expressed concerns to the North Eastern Health Board about the level of hysterectomies being carried out there by consultant obstetrician Dr Michael Neary.

A subsequent inquiry, prompted by a pressure group Patient Focus, which reported in 2006, found that Dr Neary had carried out 129 peripartum hysterectomies between 1974 and 1998. The majority of obstetricians carry out fewer than ten such hysterectomies in their careers.

The number of hysterectomies carried out was 'truly shocking' the report, by Judge Maureen Harding Clarke, said. Dr Neary had been removed from the medical register in 2003.[11]

The report's main findings include:

- Dr Neary had a 'morbid sensitivity' to bleeding in patients during surgery. He performed hysterectomies in order to prevent future bleeding.
- Dr Neary had 'a deep fault line' which was recognised early but never corrected. 'It is the story of a committed doctor with a misplaced sense of confidence in his own ability. It is a story of deep misunderstanding and misapplication of clinical evidence.'
- Nobody at the hospital or no institution dealing with the hospital raised concerns about Dr Neary's activities until two

midwives spoke to the North Eastern Health Board which had taken over the hospital from the Medical Missionaries of Mary.

- In the absence of peer reviews and other benchmarking, similar scandals can arise elsewhere in hospitals. 'Any isolated institution which fails to have in place a process of outcome review by peers and benchmark comparators can produce similar scandals as those which occurred at Lourdes Hospital.'
- The report also suggest that whistleblowers need to be given legal protection to enable them to raise legitimate concerns about clinical practice.

A compensation scheme for women affected by Dr Neary's activities was announced by the government in April 2007.

MRSA

Hospital-based infections such as MRSA (Methicillin-Resistant Staphylococcus Aureus), particularly following surgery, became a major issue from 2000 onwards. MRSA was first recorded as a cause of death by a coroner's court in November 2006. The coroner made an order that future deaths resulting from hospital infections should be reported both to the coroner and to relevant authorities to allow the compiling of statistics.[12]

The Minister for Health and Children, Mary Harney TD, told the Dáil in October 2006 that the spread of MRSA was caused mainly by over-prescribing of antibiotics though hygiene was a contributory factor.[13]

The Health Service Executive had published guidelines for hospitals on inhibiting the spread of MRSA in 2005. Measures recommended included hand hygiene, sufficient space between beds, more isolation rooms, a clean hospital environment and the avoidance of overcrowding.

Hygiene audits of hospitals began to be carried out on a national basis in 2005 and the results published.

In Ireland statistics began to be gathered in 1999 by laboratories reporting to the Health Protection Surveillance Centre. However, the statistics do not give a true picture of the absolute numbers of cases of MRSA in the country. This is because the number of laboratories increased substantially over the period and therefore the increases in cases of MRSA infection reflect the increase in the number of laboratories reporting.

In absolute figures, 592 cases of MRSA were reported in 2005 compared to 553 in 2004. Over the period 1999 to 2005, the proportion of cases of staphylococcus aureus which were methicillin-resistant has remained steady at about 40%.[14]

The Office for National Statistics in the UK in 2005 published statistics which showed that the number of deaths in which MRSA was a factor had more than doubled between 1999 and 2003.[15]

LEAS CROSS

The care of older people in nursing homes and the quality of the inspection and regulation system became controversial topics in 2005 following the broadcast of a television programme exposing conditions at the Leas Cross Nursing Home in Dublin.[16]

The broadcast, using a hidden camera, showed worrying treatment of residents including the use of Buxton chairs, a form of restraint.

The home closed shortly afterwards in 2005.

A report by Professor Desmond O'Neill, consultant geriatrician, published in 2006,[17] described the level of care provided at the home as amounting to 'institutional abuse'. It found that while the average patient transferred from the hospital to the home spent 221 days at Leas Cross, persons transferred from St Ita's Hospital, Portrane, a psychiatric hospital, to Leas Cross had a median period to death of 77 days.

He noted that, according to the records he saw, 'an alarming number' of residents were in Buxton chairs.

For a maximum number of 111 residents, medical cover was provided by one doctor at a time.

Northern Area Health Board/HSE[18] inspection reports from January 2004 were expressing concerns about Leas Cross, he wrote, and in March 2005 consultants at St Ita's Hospital had raised concerns in letters to Health Board officials.

He was critical of the failure by the health authorities to respond effectively to the concerns raised.

'Of particular concern is the lack of documentation that the NAHB/HSE (Northern Area) management responded to the very serious nature of the written concerns expressed by senior clinicians, of the very poor quality of care detected in the review of complaints by families, of the clear expression of concern by the Dublin city coroner over the death of one patient which was in the public domain and of the sustained length of time it took to appreciate that Leas Cross was not going to significantly alter its ways.'

The responsiveness of health authorities was also raised by a health consultant, Mr Martin Hynes, who stated in 2006 that in 2004 he had warned the Eastern Regional Health Authority of conditions at the home.

Following the broadcast of the RTÉ programme in 2005, the Taoiseach Mr Ahern stated that 'the government is determined that a new and stronger regulatory system will be put in place so vulnerable people, particularly the elderly, are protected.'

'The inspectorate will be independent of the HSE,' he said. 'Otherwise the HSE would be referring patients and also examining facilities. The inspectorate therefore must be independent.'[19]

More than a year later, in December 2006, the Minister for Health and Children, Mary Harney TD, stated that the Health Bill, 2006, to give effect to these undertakings, would be published and progressed speedily through the Dáil.[20]

SYMPHYSIOTOMY

The new century saw the emergence of a controversial issue concerning medical practices in the past, though the view that it was a scandal was not entirely unanimous. It concerned the practice of symphysiotomy in maternity hospitals in Ireland between the 1950s into the 1980s. The procedure involves sawing through the pubic bone either before or after the birth of the child when labour is obstructed. The aim is to widen the pelvis on a permanent basis.

According to a group called Survivors of Symphysiotomy, established with the help of the Women's Council of Ireland, many of the women who had this operation were left with acute pain, incontinence and other problems including impaired mobility. It was alleged that in many cases the procedure was carried out without the consent of the women themselves.

The Women's Council of Ireland alleged that the procedure was adopted so that the women would not need to use contraception or be sterilised. Had they not had the operation performed they would have needed repeated Caesarean sections, according to the Council.[21]

However according to a letter to *The Irish Times* by Mr Peter Boylan, a former master of Holles Street Hospital (1991–98) and by Mr Tony Farmar, author of *Holles Street 1894–1994*,[22] 'the introduction of symphysiotomy was driven not by Catholic teaching but by the medical risks associated with repeated Caesareans . . . In fact, maternal mortality was the main concern of all obstetricians in the 1940s and 1950s.'

The doctors who carried out the symphysiotomies were 'undoubtedly' influenced by Catholic teaching on sterilisation, 'but this should not be a surprise. Doctors surely have a duty of care to respect their patients' beliefs and the population served by Holles Street and the Coombe was largely comprised of working-class Catholic mothers.'[23]

The issue remained unresolved in 2006 but it shares one characteristic with other controversies mentioned in this chapter: this is that much of the anger felt by patients today arises from their belief that they were not given adequate information at the time.

CONCLUSION

The controversies and scandals of the past have led to a point at which there is a greater demand than ever before for transparency and for measures ensuring the continuing competence of doctors and others providing health services.

Partly in response to issues arising from scandals of the kind outlined above, the Minister for Health and Children, Mary Harney TD, appointed a Commission on Patient Safety and Quality Assurance which held its first meeting in January 2007. The Commission's task, she said at its first meeting, 'is to make our health system a place where the highest possible standards of patient safety and quality care are pursued and implemented rigorously by all who work in the health services.'

She added: 'While individual error may play an important part in adverse events we must examine how hospitals and other services can be managed to create an environment in which safety and quality are central to everyone's job.'[24]

It seems fair to say that the appointment of the Commission has been a considerable achievement, in particular for groups representing patients affected by various scandals—though the price paid by members has been, in some cases, extremely high in terms of ill health or death.

It is worth reflecting that one of the major problems facing the healthcare industry worldwide is how to ensure that clinical intervention is evidence-based and appropriate. Some studies in the USA suggest that only 50% of clinical interventions are properly evidence-based. It is a major problem from a health perspective and from a cost/affordability perspective. The best and perhaps only answer is a rigorous process of peer review for all branches of medicine overseen by an audit process involving significant lay involvement.

Chapter 10 ∽

HOW THE HEALTH OF THE POPULATION HAS CHANGED

INTRODUCTION

The health of the population, when measured by life expectancy at birth, has improved substantially over the past half century. Infant mortality has been very substantially reduced. Once-dreaded infectious diseases, such as tuberculosis, are of relatively little concern. Improved living standards have helped to created a general improvement in health.

But much of the improvement in life expectancy is due to the reduction in infant mortality. The life expectancy of older men has changed relatively little for the best part of a century. Cancer has joined heart disease as a major cause of death. Indeed, in relation to these diseases, our record is among the poorest in the world. The consumption of alcohol has been increasing at a remarkable rate.

Today it is individual lifestyle factors rather than the poor environmental conditions of the past that tend to be behind major diseases affecting the population. Heart disease and cancer have increased in importance as sources of ill health due in many cases to such behaviours as smoking, excessive drinking, poor diet and lack of exercise.

Historically, major improvements in the health of the popu-lation have been due to better sanitation and hygiene, greater public awareness of the value of preventive measures and the development of vaccines and other protective drugs.

Curry (2003) notes that while the health services contributed to the improved health of the population, it is difficult to isolate the precise contribution made by these services.

Measures such as the provision of public housing—a policy of governments since Independence—led to the eventual elimination of slums with their attendant health problems. For those who would otherwise have been living in slums, the implementation of housing policy may have contributed more to their physical and mental wellbeing than the health services *per se.*

ORIGINS

Most of the 19th century was characterised by outbreaks of infectious diseases which, in the words of Curry (2003), 'wrought havoc' on the population. For instance, as many as 25,000 people died in a cholera outbreak in 1832–33.

Poor nutrition, famine, overcrowding and infected water supplies all contributed to infection and to ill health during the century. High infant mortality, gastroenteritis and TB, as well as deaths from epidemics, were among the diseases that resulted from these conditions.

It was only in the later part of the century that the link between cholera and infected water was established. The Public Health Act, 1878, resulted from the establishment of this link and from the work of health reformers. The Act aimed to prevent the spread of disease by ensuring that there was proper sanitation, that water was clean and that food was safe. The measures introduced by the Act were a great success and succeeded in ending the epidemics which had been a mark of the 19th century.

Public health measures of this kind and improvements in living conditions all brought about major improvements in the health of the people. Better housing, improved nutrition and vaccination against disease, as well as the measures mentioned above, formed the backdrop to steady improvements in the health of the population in the 20th century.

In addition, the dispensary system introduced under the Poor Relief Act of 1851, in which a doctor was employed in each dispensary district to provide a free service to people below a certain income, was an important public as well as personal health measure. The dispensaries remained in operation until 1972.

Tuberculosis posed a major threat to health in the first half of the 20th century. Hensey (1979) has described TB at that time as 'probably the most feared disease in Ireland'.

In 1927, TB was killing 145 people per 100,000 of the population, most of them young people who were, in some cases, the siblings of persons who had already died from the disease. By 1957, the death-rate had fallen to 24 in 100,000. Vaccinations against tuberculosis had been introduced in 1949.

Along with TB, pneumonia, whooping cough, measles, gastroenteritis and diphtheria were leading cause of death among young children.

The Tuberculosis Act, 1945, provided for the building of sanatoria for the treatment of TB patients. Devlin points out that this, together with the free treatment and vaccination provided for under the Health Act, 1947, greatly reduced the impact of TB. The latter introduced free hospital treatment for people with infectious diseases. The number of deaths caused not only by TB but also by the other infectious diseases was quickly reduced.

BIRTHS, DEATHS AND POPULATION

All the main measures of the health of the population have shown major improvements in the half century to 2007.

When the first life table was compiled in 1926, males had a life expectancy at birth of 57.4 years and females of 57.9 years. By

1960, this had improved to 68.1 years for males and 71.9 for females. By 2002, a male baby could expect to live for 75.1 years and a female baby for 80.3 years.

This improvement was largely due to improvements in mortality rates in infants and young children. But life expectancy for older people, particularly the middle-aged and elderly remains low by European standards. This is due mainly, Devlin suggests, to premature mortality from heart disease and cancer.

Infant mortality was reduced from 68 per 1,000 live births in 1947 to 5.8 per 1,000 in 2001. Infant mortality is now due mainly to congenital abnormalities, and infections now account for less than 5% of deaths among infants. As Kelleher (1997) points out the falls in infant mortality represent a remarkable achievement given that for much of the period Ireland had higher fertility rates than the rest of Europe.[1] Child welfare clinics, school health services (introduced towards the end of the 1920s), improved welfare allowances, growing prosperity and better housing have all contributed to falls in mortality in infants and young children. Maternal mortality has fallen to two or three deaths a year.

Death-rates have improved significantly and there have been some changes in causes of death. Cancer caused about 11% of deaths in 1950 and 25% in 2001. Heart disease continues to be the main cause of death. It is notable that over a period of almost 50 years between 1947 and 1995, the proportion of deaths caused by heart or heart-related disease remained at 25%. Our rates of cardiovascular disease and of cancer are among the highest in the world for men and women.

The birth-rate has shown interesting and sometimes unexpected changes over the past half century. In 1960, the birth-rate was 21.5% per thousand of the population. This fell to a low of 13.5% in 1995. It then began to rise again and stood at 15.3% in 2004.

Emigration saw the population fall from 3.2 million in 1901 to a historic low of 2.8 million in 1961. It took until 1971 for the population (2.98 million) to recover to the 1926 level. Thereafter there was a steady rise and it stood at 3.9 million in 2002.

A consequence of emigration was the slow ageing of the population. The proportion of the population aged 60 years or older was 15% in 2002 and this was expected to rise to 28% in 2050.[2] By contrast, 21% of the population of the UK was over 60 in 2001.[3]

While life expectancy as measured from birth has improved, Kelleher points out that life expectancy for older men has not improved since the 1920s. The life expectancy for males at 55 (23.4 years) was only 4.3 years higher in 2002 than it was in 1926. For women, life expectancy at 55 has increased by 7.8 years to 27.4 years according to Central Statistics Office figures.[4] On the positive side, the dramatic decreases in infant mortality (see previous page) mean that many, many more people actually reach old age.

HEALTH PROMOTION AND PUBLIC HEALTH

The importance of health promotion received growing recognition during the 1980s. The Department of Health document, *Health: The Wider Dimensions* (1986), saw health as an issue which reflected more aspects of life than could be addressed within the health sector.[5] In this, the Department was echoing the views of the Health Education Bureau in its 1987 report, *Promoting Health through Public Policy.*[6]

NUI Galway established a Chair of Health Promotion in 1990 with funding from the Department of Health. As Kelleher points out, this was an innovative development internationally and in Irish terms.

The national health strategies published in 1994, *Shaping a Healthier Future,*[7] and in 2001, *Quality and Fairness, A Health System for You,*[8] emphasised the importance of better health and better quality of life, and not just the treating of sickness, as objects of health policy.

Nevertheless, health promotion has played a secondary role to medical care, particularly hospital care, throughout the period.

Kelleher suggests that a bias towards institutional care owed something at least to the availability of buildings (such as workhouses and their associated infirmaries) from the period after the Famine on which the county hospital network was based. In addition, the availability of Irish Sweeps money, especially in the 1930s and 1940s, led to an increase in the provision of hospital buildings.

The Health Education Bureau was established in 1975. Its members were appointed by the Minister for Health and it was responsible for organising programmes of health education. It also aimed to coordinate the work of voluntary bodies already engaged in health education in various fields. Non-governmental organisations such as the Irish Cancer Society and the Irish Heart Foundation did invaluable work in promoting healthier lifestyles.

Kelleher points out that the Bureau did not have links in any formal way with health boards or other agencies and these tended to work separately on public health issues.

The document *Promoting Health Through Public Policy* (1987) was produced by a working party established by the Health Education Bureau. It emphasised that various sectors and bodies must work together if significant improvements were to be made in relation to avoidable diseases.

In 1988, the Health Promotion Unit of the Department of Health replaced the Health Education Bureau, a cabinet sub-committee on health promotion was formed and the National Advisory Council on Health Promotion was set up.

This Council was replaced by a new advisory body chaired by a junior minister on the publication of *Shaping a Healthier Future*.

Health boards continued to develop health promotion policies often in conjunction with the schools. The 1990s saw the appointment of health promotion officers in most health boards and also the appointment of directors of public health. The latter were responsible for disease surveillance and planning among other duties.

The NUI Galway's Centre for Health Promotion Studies has undertaken research on a wide variety of public health issues including the health needs of travellers and of carers, and attitudes towards health and wellbeing.

NATIONAL DISEASE SURVEILLANCE

Surveillance of trends in infectious disease is a key public health function. The National Disease Surveillance Centre was established for this purpose in 1998. It became part of the Health Service Executive as the Health Protection Surveillance Centre when the HSE was set up in 2005.

The aim of HPSC is to collate, interpret and disseminate data on infectious disease. This is achieved through surveillance and independent advice, epidemiological investigation, research and training.[9]

HPSC has the following main areas of responsibility: surveillance of major communicable diseases; providing expert advice and support to HSE departments of public health and hospitals; training; research; making policy recommendations to government departments and agencies; and providing information on infectious diseases to the public and the media.

THE BATTLE AGAINST TOBACCO

A ban on smoking in the workplace was introduced in Ireland in 2004. Announcing the ban, the Minister for Health, Micheál Martin TD, stated that: 'Almost 70% of the adult population in Ireland are non-smokers yet many people are unwillingly exposed, on a daily basis, to toxic environmental tobacco smoke. Many public areas and facilities and some workplaces are subject to prohibitions and restrictions on smoking and there is a growing demand for increased protection from environmental tobacco smoke. Opinion polls here show there is enormous public support, almost 90%, for extending bans on environmental tobacco smoke.'[10]

At the time of the introduction of the ban, an estimated 7,000 people were dying from smoking-related diseases every year. The cost of health services for smokers was estimated at €1 billion per annum. On average, smokers lost 10–15 years from their life expectancy.

ALCOHOL CONSUMPTION

As a public health problem, excessive consumption of alcohol has been a feature of Irish society for well over a century. Ferriter (2004) noted that in 1891–92 there were what he called an 'astounding' 100,528 arrests for drunkenness.[11] Publicans proliferated in this atmosphere. Tralee in Co. Kerry had 117 pubs for a population of 9,367 people.

When the *Titanic* sank in 1912, the founder of the Pioneer Association, Father James Cullen, wrote in the *Irish Catholic* that 'thousands all around us are perishing in the ocean of drink, and cry in vain for those who can, but will not, help them' (Ferriter, 2004).

In 1961, St John of God opened a special unit for alcoholics in Dublin. A substantial proportion of those admitted to psychiatric hospitals were there because of drinking or to 'dry out' as the process is colloquially described.

Consumption of alcohol increased dramatically at the beginning of the new century. The *Interim Report of the Strategic Task Force on Alcohol* (2002)[12] reported that between 1989 and 1999, alcohol consumption per capita in Ireland increased by 41%, while ten of the EU member states showed a decrease. In 2000, alcohol consumption per adult in Ireland was 14.2 litres, whereas the EU average was 9.1 litres of pure alcohol per capita. In six years to 2002, the consumption of spirits increased by over 50% and there had been an increase of 100% in the consumption of cider.

ILLEGAL DRUG USE

Drug abuse has been a public health concern since the early 1970s. The abuse of heroin has been a particular concern, especially in Dublin. Estimates of the number of heroin addicts range from 6,000 to 13,000. A total of 7,559 people sought treatment between 1990 and 1999 for problems arising from addiction to heroin or other opiate-related drugs.[13] Other drugs which began to be abused increasingly from the 1970s onwards included cannabis, MDMA ('ecstasy') and cocaine.

In 1996, the *First Report of the Ministerial Task Force on Measures to Reduce the Demand for Drugs* established the National Drug Strategy Team and the Local Drugs Task Forces in twelve areas of Dublin and one in Cork City.[14]

AIDS

A new threat to the health of the population came in the 1980s with the development of HIV and AIDS.

Initially, HIV led inevitably to AIDS and AIDS led inevitably to death. Public health authorities feared an epidemic of AIDS and of AIDS-related deaths.[15] However, the development of effective therapies during the 1990s meant that HIV became a chronic, controllable infection rather than a death sentence. Between 1982 and the end of 1999, there was a total of 691 reported cases of AIDS and 349 reported deaths.

The main routes of transmission of HIV were sex between men and IV drug use. One of the strongest motives for the establishment of Local Drugs Task Forces and other services for IV drug users was to reduce the spread of HIV infection. Transmission of HIV among IV drug users was substantially reduced (from 41.4% of new infections in 1992 to 21.5% in 1998) according to figures for the period 1993 to 1998.[16]

The Gay Men's Health Project was established in Dublin in 1992 by the Eastern Health Board to provide a range of sexual health services including screening, counselling and distribution of condoms. State funding was provided for outreach workers in Cork, Galway and Limerick. The Gay Men's Health Network was established in 1994 to enable voluntary and statutory groups involved in sexual health issues for gay and bisexual men to work together. Despite these efforts, the National AIDS Strategy Committee noted in its 2002 report that the transmission of HIV among gay men had remained steady.[17]

BREASTCHECK

In an effort to reduce mortality from breast cancer, the BreastCheck programme began offering free breast screening to women aged 50–64 in the Eastern Regional Health Authority, North Eastern and Midlands Health Board areas in February 2000. Screening was later extended to Carlow, Kilkenny and Wexford. In 2006, planning applications were lodged for new BreastCheck Clinical Units in Cork and Galway.[18]

CONCLUSION

Better health services, better preventive services and a healthier economy have all contributed to improvements in the health of the population, Devlin (1997) suggests.[19]

But the failure to substantially improve the life expectancy of older men, the persistence of heart disease as the main cause of death and the continuing rise in alcohol consumption left a great deal of work to be done in the new century.

PART TWO

Vhi HEALTHCARE

INTRODUCTION

Although the VHI was established in relatively modern times, the society into which it was introduced is scarcely recognisable today. The economy was poor. Emigration had blighted much of the country, especially along the western seaboard. In 1957, Ireland was the only country in Europe in which the consumption of goods and services fell (Ferriter, 2004).[1]

In some respects, the health system had changed little since the previous century and would not change radically for another fifteen years. In most parts of the country, public health services were administered on a county basis. Persons who could not afford to pay for a general practitioner services attended dispensaries, often dating from the 19th century, and were segregated from those who could afford to attend their doctor's own surgery.

Entitlement to hospital services was based on income; up to 15% of the population was judged, in a relatively poor country, to have an income above the limit for free hospital services. This provided the impetus for the establishment of the VHI. From the beginning, though, the VHI drew members not only from those who had no public entitlement but from many who had.

It was not until the 1970s that a modern system of health administration was introduced in Ireland. Over the following decades, entitlement to free hospital services was extended to the entire population. Nevertheless, the VHI continued to flourish. The private system could offer quicker access to many more treatments than the public system; choice of consultant; members could avoid lengthy waiting periods for hospital beds and they had the option of semi-private or private accommodation.[2]

Traditionally, private patients have tended to be treated in beds allocated for that purpose in public or voluntary hospitals. For the past twenty years the ratio of treatment in public versus private hospitals has been approximately 50:50 and it is now increasing towards the private hospital area.

It was not all plain sailing for the VHI. The late 1980s and early 1990s saw the organisation facing a major threat from a combination of the increasing cost of medical care and a refusal by the government to authorise certain price increases. That challenge was met successfully. New challenges followed: the introduction of competition into the health insurance market highlighted the community rated funding model, adopted by Vhi Healthcare since 1957 but which was now required by legislation. The legislation also provided for risk equalisation, a system of transfer payments, designed to underpin community rating. This was not activated until 2006, placing severe financial constraints on the organisation. To date, no transfers have taken place and the legal and political debate continues.

As its first half-century ended, Vhi Healthcare found itself in a position that had changed utterly. Government policies encouraging the building of private hospitals meant substantial changes in the infrastructure through which private services were delivered. This, in turn, was expected to mean higher costs for health insurers and their members. The future relationship between the public and private systems and the implications of this for people with private health insurance, were still only emerging. And Vhi Healthcare had a remarkable membership of over 1.57 million members which meant it covered almost half the population 50 years after it was founded and a decade after the introduction of competition.

ORIGINS

Private health insurance existed in Ireland prior to the establishment of the VHI. However, it never caught the public imagination in the same way that the VHI was to do and its predecessors in the marketplace met with little success in this regard.[3]

Insurance companies such as the Insurance Corporation of Ireland offered private medical insurance but this and other private schemes ran into difficulties, partly because of the lack of public interest and partly because of the cost of meeting claims for pre-existing illnesses (Taylor, 1997).[4] In addition, the British insurer, Private Patients Plan, had a small number of members recruited through brokers but its membership never reached a significant level.[5] At this time Western Provident Association, another British insurer, was also in the Irish market and remained until 1963–64. Its membership was comprised of civil servants and bank officials from all of the main banks at the time.

The 1953 Health Act recognised three categories of people in relation to entitlement to health services. Persons judged unable to provide health services for themselves and their dependants were entitled to a comprehensive service free of charge. The middle income group was entitled to somewhat more restricted services free of charge or at a modest charge. Members of the higher income group were obliged to meet all their own health-care costs. People in this group—about 15% of the population— could obtain free public hospital services only if they could show that meeting the cost themselves would involve undue hardship.

Ryan (2006) suggests that this income-related system owed much to the opposition of the Catholic Church and of the medical profession to what they saw as 'the ghastly march of State medicine.'[6] Indeed, the Act had become law in the shadow of the Mother and Child controversy which saw the Minister for Health, Dr Noel Browne, resign in 1952 following a battle with the Church and medical profession on the issue of State involvement in medicine.[7]

In addition, the economy was in poor shape, emigration was high and the population was falling.[8] This, too, limited what could be done in terms of the provision of free health services.

In these circumstances, the Minister for Health, T.F. O'Higgins TD, set up an Advisory Body in 1955 to examine the feasibility of a voluntary private health insurance scheme.

The idea of establishing a private health insurance scheme on a national scale had been put to Mr O'Higgins' predecessor, Dr Jim Ryan, by the Irish Medical Association. Dr Ryan had not taken up the proposal.

The Advisory Body was chaired by H.B. O'Hanlon, then Taxing Master of the High Court. Its membership included Dublin surgeon T.C.J. O'Connell, representing the Irish Medical Association.

Under its terms of reference, the body was to advise the Minister for Health as to the feasibility of introducing a scheme of voluntary insurance to enable citizens to insure themselves and their dependants against the cost of hospital treatment, dental services and the provision of medical or surgical appliances.

It is interesting to note that the target group, as envisaged in the terms of reference, included any citizens who wished to insure themselves and their dependants—and not only those who were ineligible for free hospital services.

Nevertheless, as Taylor suggests, the members of the advisory group 'must have been somewhat apprehensive at previous unsuccessful attempts by commercial insurers to continue with schemes, in particular the Insurance Corporation of Ireland who withdrew theirs after a few years, having at first increased premiums by 50%.'

The enticement, however, of income tax relief as provided in the 1955 Finance Act and the success of voluntary health insurance in other European countries encouraged them to recommend a scheme to the Minister for Health (Taylor, 1997).

In its report, published in 1956, the Advisory Body concluded that it was feasible to introduce 'a scheme of voluntary insurance against the cost of hospital maintenance, of surgical and medical services in hospital and of maternity.' It was not practical, it decided, to include benefit for general practitioner services or for normal dental services in the scheme.[9]

It suggested that the best type of organisation to administer such a scheme was a non-profit-making company. Such a company should be exempted from obligations concerning share capital and other obligations which normally applied under insurance law.

The Advisory Body had a two-fold rationale for suggesting that the scheme be administered by an organisation established by the State:

> We are not aware that there are any interests in this country prepared to establish a health insurance scheme of the kind mentioned in our terms of reference and if a scheme is to be introduced, the State must take the initiative. A scheme could be administered by a Department of State, but we think it would have a wider appeal to the public if it were administered by a company such as we describe.[10]

Interestingly, it stated that 'a voluntary health insurance scheme is unlikely to have any appreciable effect on the finances of voluntary hospitals.'

ESTABLISHMENT OF THE VHI

The Voluntary Health Insurance Board was appointed on 12 February 1957, under the Voluntary Health Insurance Act, 1957.

Following the publication of the Advisory Body's report, the Minister had consulted with the trade unions, the medical profession and other interested parties. In agreeing to the establishment of the VHI, the government rejected one of the recommendations of the Advisory Body: there should be no benefit for maternity costs, it decided, on the grounds that maternity was not an illness and therefore could be budgeted for.

The thinking behind the introduction of the scheme was explained by the Minister to the Dáil in the following terms, when introducing the second stage of the Voluntary Health Insurance Bill in November 1956:

> The aim of such an insurance scheme is to help people to help themselves. This idea of self-reliance is fundamental, and unless the proposal is received on this understanding, it cannot operate successfully. The cost of our present services has been such as to tax the resources both of central and local funds, and the time has surely come when further expansion must be along the lines of making it easier for participants to fend for themselves. I hope that it will be possible to create a worthwhile public opinion behind this idea of voluntary health insurance, a public opinion expressive of the determination of our people to preserve our natural dignity as individuals and at the same time to make prudent provision for the hazards of ill health.[11]

The proposal was supported by deputies who included Mr Seán Flanagan, later Minister for Health, and Dr Patrick Hillery, later President. The Bill was endorsed unanimously by the Dáil on 29 November 1956 and sent to the Senate which approved it without amendment. It became law on 5 February 1957.

The VHI was granted a near monopoly by the Act. Only those health insurance schemes which were provided by a trade union or by a society registered in the State before the passing of the 1957 Act under the Friendly Societies Acts were allowed to continue.

The board of the VHI met for the first time on 19 February 1957. In his address to the first meeting the Minister, Mr O'Higgins, referred to arguments which had been made against the establishment of the VHI:

There are those who say that voluntary health insurance simply would not work here; others claimed that the State should provide health services for the whole of the population. I see no reason why we should not be able to do here what has been done successfully in other countries. There is no doubt that there is a demand for health insurance facilities among a large section of the community. If that demand is met in a reasonable, efficient and sympathetic way—and I am sure that you will meet it in that way—I am quite confident that those who are sceptical of the success of voluntary health insurance here will be eventually silenced.

As to the claim that the State should provide health services for all, I said on more than one occasion while the Bill was going through the Dáil and Senate, that I believed strongly that it would be contrary to our ideals and traditions that the State should supplant individual effort unless there are grounds for believing that the individual himself cannot himself meet his responsibilities. The whole aim of this health insurance scheme is to help people to help themselves; the idea of self-reliance is fundamental to it. Indeed, I take some satisfaction in having sponsored a piece of legislation which enables an important social service to be made available without imposing any burden on the taxpayer or ratepayer.

He went on to encourage the VHI not to confine itself to those who had no entitlement to free health services but to develop a market among those who did have such an eligibility:

I am convinced that there are many such people who would prefer to cover their health hazards through insurance rather than through the services provided under the Act. Those, for instance, who would prefer to make their own hospital arrangements instead of accepting the arrangements made by the health authorities are likely to be sympathetic to the idea of health insurance. You will have done a good day's work if you can succeed in attracting into your schemes a number of persons eligible under the Health Act in such a way as to relieve the State and the health authorities of their cost under the Act in respect of those persons. It is significant that in Great Britain, in spite of the existence of the National Health Scheme, the number of persons taking up voluntary health insurance has grown tremendously over the last few years.

And referring to the VHI's monopoly he had this to say:

I did not consider that there was room for more than one organisation to operate successfully in the rather limited market we have here and I proposed to issue licences only to those concerns which are not likely to be in serious competition with you. I am glad that it has been possible to ease your difficulties by giving you more or less a clear field to operate in. The fact that you would have to manage your affairs without making a profit or incurring a loss would, in any event, have made it difficult for you to work on a competitive basis.

I am very much aware that this project you are undertaking is an experiment. You will be, in a sense, sailing into uncharted seas. I have great faith, however, in the future of voluntary health insurance in this country and I shall follow with great interest its development in your hands.

Regarding Mr O'Higgins' reference to 'what has been done successfully in other countries' it is interesting to note that, shortly before his death in 2003, he told the Chief Executive of the VHI, Mr Vincent Sheridan, that the VHI and the legislation under which it was established had been based on the system in Australia.[12]

The first chairman of the VHI was Mr James Troy, an accountant, who was also on the board of the Richmond, the Coombe, the Royal Hospital Donnybrook and the Irish Hospitals Trust. Mr Troy chaired the VHI from 1957 to 1982. The members of the first board included Mr T.C.J. O'Connell, senior consultant surgeon at St Vincent's Hospital. Mr O'Connell had been president of the Irish Medical Association in 1955 and had been a member of the Advisory Body. In the year the VHI was founded, he was vice-chairman of the National Health Council. He was president of An Bord Altranais and a member of the National Blood Transfusion Service Board. He remained on the board of the VHI for 26 years (Taylor, 1997).

The other board members were Mssrs H.B. O'Hanlon, M.P. Linehan and P.J. Shaw.

The VHI opened to the public on 2 October 1957 with about a dozen staff. Its General Manager was Mr Noel Burke. The first public offices of the VHI were at Nos. 8 and 9 South Leinster Street where Mr Bob Graham (later Deputy General Manager) recalled staff at work sitting on wooden boxes surrounded by rolls of linoleum.[13] The office later expanded to include No. 7 South Leinster Street before moving to the present premises at 20 Lower Abbey Street, Dublin.

The first General Manager, Noel Burke, had worked for the Norwich Union and the Caledonian Insurance Company prior to his appointment. He died at 48 years of age in 1965. At the time he was a member of the Peamount Hospital board. He had also been chairman of the National Organisation for Rehabilitation, later renamed the National Rehabilitation Board.

The Minister, Mr O'Higgins, loaned the new organisation £13,000 to get it started. When the inter-party government fell in 1957 and Fianna Fáil returned to power, he was succeeded by

Mr Seán MacEntee. Mr O'Connell later informed Ms Ruth Barrington that Mr MacEntee threatened to shut down the VHI unless it was financially independent within a year. However, the VHI was a quick success and paid back the loan by the due date (Barrington, 1987).[14]

The board, in its planning, anticipated a membership of 500,000 which was the figure estimated by the Advisory Body. By February 1958, the VHI already had 23,238 members and this number grew to 53,139 the following year and 78,778 in 1960. Membership reached 500,000 in 1973.

EARLY SCHEMES

In its first year of business, the VHI offered three schemes to the public. Scheme A covered the cost of private rooms in public hospitals; Scheme B covered the cost of semi-private beds in all private hospitals; and Scheme C covered the cost of private rooms in all private hospitals. The cost of an annual subscription to Scheme A for an adult was £3.15s, Scheme B cost £5 and Scheme C £7. A married couple with four or more children would pay £13.10s for annual membership of Scheme A, £17.10s for annual membership of Scheme B and £23.10s for Scheme C. Persons aged 60 and over paid an extra 15% (Taylor, 1997).

Group subscriptions were offered at a discount from the beginning.

In its second year, the VHI began a gradual process of extending the period for which maintenance benefit was paid. Maintenance charges were an important issue because the length of stay in hospital tended to be long by today's standards.

Taylor (1997) cites the example of an in-patient with a tumour who, in 1958, might spend as long as two months in hospital at a cost of almost £120. Of this, the surgeon's fee would account for £20 and the maintenance charge for just over £74. Benefits payable under Scheme A would have left a shortfall of £26 on these charges, while Scheme B would cover all but £5.

In the early days the VHI was very well aware that its predecessors, including the Insurance Corporation of Ireland, had had
difficulties with their medical insurance schemes because of
claims for treatment for pre-existing illnesses.

The VHI placed restrictions on cover for pre-existing conditions. It also, in its earliest years, reserved the right to withdraw
cover for illnesses which emerged following the taking of
membership and which gave rise to recurrent claims. In practice,
this withdrawal of cover for chronic or recurrent illnesses was
never implemented and the provision was later dropped.[15] Age
limits were also abolished.

The VHI was a success from the start. Success, however, had
been by no means assured, as Mr Leonard McGloughlin, who was
a member of the underwriting staff from the start and became
Development Manager in 1967, later wrote:

In 1957, when the schemes were in the planning stage, there
were many prophets of doom to say that such a project could
not succeed in Ireland, supporting their arguments with
references to the disaster which had overtaken previous efforts
by commercial interests to underwrite this type of business.

An Irishman's traditional attitude to insurance in general
was presented as the final nail in the coffin of any health
insurance scheme.

That their gloomy prognostications came to nought is now a
matter of history, but it must not be forgotten that in the
critical first years of the scheme the screening of applicants
acted as an effective cushion against the effects of adverse
selection against the Board. The very real problems of this
period of establishment were surmounted by what can best be
described as a combination of astute underwriting practice
backed by a vigorous sales and public relations campaign. That
so many subscribers were prepared to accept the Board's terms
in good faith even in cases where only restricted cover was

offered, is to my mind most significant . . . (McGloughlin in Taylor, 1997).[16]

Why did the VHI succeed where others had failed? According to Graham,[17] there were five major factors behind its success:

- The VHI was Irish.
- The VHI was non-profit making.
- The medical profession strongly supported it.
- The private hospitals were in favour.
- VHI staff travelled the country and promoted it directly in companies and other organisations.

McGloughlin suggests the growth in membership in the early decades was spurred by the needs of the upper income group who had no public entitlement and by the attractiveness to the middle income group of being able to choose their own specialist and of private and semi-private accommodation.[18] A public hospital ward at that time contained many beds and little or no privacy.

That the resumption of substantial membership growth in the late 1980s and early 1990s coincided with health service cutbacks suggests that speedy access to treatment was also a motivator, in the later period at any rate.

STEADY EXPANSION

Membership grew steadily, from 23,238 in 1958 to 321,777 in 1968 and 645,165 in 1978. The pace of growth slowed in the 1980s, a period of economic uncertainty and high unemployment but nevertheless membership exceeded one million for the first time in 1983. There was a slight fall in membership in 1986 but growth resumed again in 1987 when particularly deep health cuts were being implemented by a new government.

The VHI expanded both in membership and in location. It opened branch offices in Cork in 1959, in Limerick in 1970, in Galway also in 1970 and in Dun Laoghaire in 1981.

According to Mr Michael Collins-Powell, who managed the Cork office, the VHI was relatively unknown to the general public in the early days as little had been spent on publicity. As might be expected, it was senior managers and others who had no entitlement to public services who were most aware of the VHI.

Mr Collins-Powell travelled his region 'by bicycle, bus and train' to meet prospective customers. Though he was attempting to establish a base for the VHI in a very large region, he was without a company car for the first few years.

His contacts usually were accounts staff as few, if any, companies had personnel departments at the time. Through these contacts he arranged to give lectures to staff on the benefits of joining the VHI.

On Friday nights he could be 'anywhere from West Cork to Waterford' giving talks to branches of farmers' organisations and community groups.

The weekend might be spent running a stand at an agricultural show or at other events which provided an opportunity to promote the VHI.

It was, he recalled, 'fairly hard going.'

As happened elsewhere in the country with growing industrial development, the arrival of increasing numbers of US companies in the area boosted membership as these companies were already used to the concept of subsidising health plans for employees.[19]

Pivotal to the success of the VHI then as now were the group schemes adopted by companies and other organisations. Within each company or other organisation, the group scheme was administered by an employee who took on the task of group secretary. Writing in the late 1960s, McGloughlin noted that there were 1,200 group secretaries and he described these as 'a band of active promoters throughout the country' (McGloughlin in Taylor, 1997).[20]

The VHI put considerable effort into cultivating the secretaries of group schemes:

It has been the practice of the Voluntary Health Insurance to arrange meetings of all group secretaries, with a view to keeping them up-to-date with the developments and thinking, and of giving them an opportunity of raising any points regarding our plans or administration. This innovation was one which was particularly appreciated and which set Voluntary Health Insurance apart in the sense that it emphasised the nature of the organisation, where those in the scheme were not only subscribers but members of a society with the common aim of mutual help.

The administrative work which running a group scheme involved for these group secretaries all had to be done manually at a time when computers were virtually unknown in Irish business. 'It's only a matter of drawing another column in the ledger' was Mr McGloughlin's reassurance to prospective customers worried about the amount of work involved![21]

In the early days of the VHI, the sale of group memberships to the civil service and other large bodies of customers such as national school teachers provided a powerful boost to the new organisation, according to Mr Brian Savage, Chief Executive from 1971 to 1979.[22]

And in what was then a largely agricultural country, encouraging people in rural areas to take out health insurance was an important marketing objective. As mentioned on the previous page in the context of Munster, employees of the VHI addressed meetings of such bodies as the Irish Countrywomen's Association and the National Farmers' Association to promote the benefits of membership. Their efforts appear to have met with some success. Mr McGloughlin wrote:

The results of such meetings must be looked for in the long term, but the steadily growing membership of the National Farmers' Association group is an indication of their efficacy.

Mr McGloughlin also touched on the issue of fees paid to doctors.

> Traditionally, medical fees have been negotiated between doctor and patient, and the doctor's criterion was the patient's capacity to pay. Obviously, to assess fees in such circumstances was anything but an exact science, and the method seemed to allow a generous margin of error.
>
> For voluntary health patients, their capacity to pay is no longer a matter of conjecture nor indeed need there be any margin for bad debts. Far too often one hears of doctors 'rubbing it in' to Voluntary Health patients, and such stories must harm the image of both the Voluntary Health Insurance scheme and indeed the medical profession as well. Here surely is a problem of education which must be met and faced. While it is important that the Voluntary Health Insurance Board avoids anything that might appear to be fee-fixing for the doctor, it is equally vital that every effort is made to bring about a rational approach to the scheme in the matter of charges generally. What is overlooked is that the insured is entitled to indemnity up to the amount of cover, and not automatically to the maximum benefits.

The State 'played a part in promoting voluntary health insurance by offering income tax concessions and subsidies towards the cost of private accommodation but the major credit must go to the Board and its highly efficient supporting staff,' the Minister for Health and Social Welfare, Charles Haughey TD, said when opening a new public office for the VHI in 1979. The context for the relationship between the State and the VHI, as outlined by Mr Haughey, was that the VHI 'is charged with providing health insurance for those who require it on a non-profit-making basis while at the same time ensuring that the Board's operations are at all times solvent.' When the VHI was established, 'there was no guarantee of success' and 'there was then little experience in this country of carrying on health insurance on a widespread scale.'[23]

INTERNATIONAL LINKS

The VHI took the initiative in the establishment of the International Federation of Voluntary Health Service Funds, now the International Federation of Health Plans. The Federation was officially inaugurated in Sydney, Australia in 1968, and the VHI has always played a role in this body—since the establishment of the Federation the chief executive of VHI has always been a member of the Council of the Federation.

According to Taylor (1997) the motivation for VHI's involvement in this move was the desirability of learning from the experience of others.

In 1966, the VHI hosted a conference in Dublin of represent-atives of international funds and it was agreed to work out a constitution and to meet again in two years' time. At the sub-sequent meeting in Sydney, in 1968, the Federation was instituted. Its purpose was the exchange of ideas and experiences about independent health services. Thereafter the Federation held a biennial conference.

In 1972, members of the Federation agreed to accept each other's customers on favourable terms. The Federation grew to become a major source of information exchange on development trends and best practice between health funds. The first Irishman to become president of the Federation (1992 to 1994) was VHI Chief Executive Tom Ryan who recalled that the Federation was 'a terrific sounding board' for the VHI in assessing issues and ideas.[24]

The VHI also supplied the Federation with an administrative director, Mr John O'Mahony who had been first secretary to the board of the VHI and had become general manager in 1965. In 1971 he resigned to become full-time administrative director of the Federation. VHI House then became the headquarters of the

Federation. Mr O'Mahony was also a member of the boards of our Lady's Hospital for Sick Children, St Luke's and the Mater Hospital. He was a member of the National Health Council and of Comhairle na nOspidéal.

Ms Frances Shiels was seconded from the VHI as his assistant. Like Mr O'Mahony she had already been involved in the work of the Federation. She became publicity manager of the VHI in 1979 and retained this post until she retired in 1994.

The offices of the Federation were at VHI House until 1978.

SCHEMES EXPANDED IN THE 1960s

Throughout its history, the VHI has extended the cover it provides to suit new circumstances either by including additional areas or removing restrictions. For instance, in 1966, hospital maintenance cover was extended from 20 to 30 weeks and the upper age limit for members was raised from 75 to 80 years. The age limit was later dropped.

This and other improvements were financed by introducing a £5 excess to in-patient hospital claims but the excess was dropped in 1970 (Taylor, 1997).

A major improvement in cover took place in 1967 when the schemes were expanded to cover prescribed drugs and medicines outside hospital, improved maternity benefits, expenses incurred for newly-born children and home nursing. The drugs and medicines scheme was to prove popular but costly and would be dropped in the 1980s.

Nineteen-sixty-seven also saw an extension from 30 weeks to 40 weeks in any one year of the maximum period of cover for hospital and nursing home maintenance charges. The upper age limit for continuing insurance was removed. Restrictions on cover for pre-existing illnesses were modified following five years' membership and removed following ten years' membership. In 1975 restrictions were removed following five years' continuous membership.

THE 1970s AND RISING COSTS

Rising claims costs became a continuing concern in the 1970s. Inflation was rampant for much of the decade. In 1974, the Consumer Price Index rose by 17%. This was followed by a rise of 20.9% in 1975 and 18% the following year.[25]

The government introduced sharp increases in the cost of private beds in public hospitals in the early 1970s. The cost of claims and of administration exceeded subscription income during 1973 and 1974. These losses were partly offset by investment income; some investments were sold. In 1975, the National Prices Commission approved a subscription increase of 15% due to a combination of inflation and increasing claims.

Nevertheless, the cover offered to members continued to change and develop. From 1977, the age loading which had been applied to the Home Scheme for persons over 60 was abolished. By now the VHI had two major schemes. The Hospital Scheme provided the traditional hospital cover. The Home Scheme covered prescribed drugs and medicines, home nursing, medical appliances and deep x-ray therapy.

In 1979 VHI decided to guarantee that hospital and nursing home charges would be fully covered, provided a patient occupied the type of accommodation for which insurance had been arranged.

Under this new indemnity principle, Taylor (1997) notes, the Board absorbed the high level of inflation in hospital charges throughout the insurance year. As subscription rates could be changed only at the annual renewal dates, this required the Board to maintain a benefit reserve.

The provision of full indemnity for hospital charges had been prompted by changes in general entitlements to hospital services. In 1978, the Minister for Health and Social Welfare, Charles Haughey TD, announced a broadening of eligibility for public hospital services. This came into effect on 6 April 1979. The new right to free hospital maintenance and treatment applied to all except to those whose income exceeded £5,500 per annum and to farmers with valuations in excess of £60. These latter two groups were required to pay professional fees even if treated in a public ward.

With most members now entitled to have hospitalisation and treatment costs covered fully as public patients in a public ward, demand grew for the VHI, too, to provide full indemnity for all costs (Taylor, 1997). The VHI responded by replacing its maintenance units system (in which the level of cover for hospital maintenance depended on the number of 'units' bought by the member) with three plans, A, B and C which guaranteed cover against hospital bills within selected accommodation categories. The new packages included, for the first time, benefit for maternity and convalescent care. A requirement that a member spend 24 hours in hospital before receiving cover for scheduled surgical or invasive medical procedures was removed. All members who joined the new hospital plans also became entitled, automatically, to a range of out-patient and domiciliary benefits.

While hospital charges were fully covered by the three plans, members were obliged to buy additional 'fee units' to cover some or all of their consultants' fees. The number of such units bought was left to the discretion of the individual member. The higher the number, the greater the cover for professional fees. The 'units' system had been introduced in 1962.

The VHI also introduced a plan, in the light of the 1979 changes, for persons who wished to be treated in a public ward but whose income obliged them to pay consultants' fees.

During 1979/80 the VHI enjoyed an almost 21% increase in membership to a total of 843,309 persons. This represents an increase in membership of 145,963 and made it a record year. The previous year, 1978/79, had also been a record year with an increase of 52,181 persons.

DEVELOPMENTS IN PRIVATE HEALTHCARE

In the 1970s and early 1980s, a number of important developments were in train in relation to the provision of private hospital care, an area which had seen little development for many years.

In 1974, the Religious Sisters of Charity had established St Vincent's Private Hospital beside St Vincent's University Hospital. In the following year, Mount Carmel Hospital in Dublin installed a sterile air theatre and joint replacement unit, a move which Mr James Sheehan, one of the developers of Blackrock Clinic, subsequently described as the beginning of the modernisation of the private hospital sector (Taylor, 1997).

The Mater Hospital was drawing up plans to build a new private hospital at Eccles Street in Dublin. Across the city, consultants were planning the establishment of Blackrock Clinic.

The Bon Secours Sisters had been working in Ireland since the late 19th century and had established a number of private hospitals. Today Bon Secours Ireland has hospitals in Cork, Dublin, Galway and Tralee.

But the private sector also included hospitals which were, in effect, nursing homes and it was clear that there was scope for development. By 1980 the VHI had taken the view that it should, itself, become involved in developing private hospitals. It made submissions to the Minister for Health in 1980 and again in 1982 seeking permission for this move.

The arguments put forward by the VHI were summarised as follows by Taylor (1997):

• Existing private facilities were in many cases obsolete and needed replacing. Some, such as the Jervis Street Private Nursing Home, were due for closure. If foreign-based healthcare organisations came into the market, they would build expensive modern hospitals without co-ordinated planning of bed numbers, location and specialities. In some cases, these hospitals would be run for profit.

- If new hospitals were built by the VHI, the location and timing of hospitals could be managed so as to minimise the impact on VHI subscriptions. Ongoing costs could be kept as low as possible through modern management practices.
- The VHI submission foresaw a situation in which private beds would be lost to the system through closure of private hospitals run by religious orders weakened by falling vocations, a lack of funding or a decision to focus on other social services. An agency such as the VHI could take over and manage these hospitals, it was argued.
- Then as now, government policy favoured the development of private facilities on the sites of major teaching hospitals. The VHI argued that it was, itself, best placed to own and finance such facilities. Its members included persons of all ages, it argued, and it was keen to cater for the special needs of each group, from childhood to old age.

The VHI put its proposals to the Minister for Health, Dr Michael Woods, in 1980. It made a further submission in July 1982. By now the VHI was insuring one million people.

However, there was no welcome for the VHI proposal in the Department of Health. As Mr Brian Dennis, Chairman from 1982 to 1987 and a Board member for 25 years recalled:

> The Department of Health was not in favour of us becoming involved at all. The Department would not support our view that at least if we went in there we would have some chance of controlling costs.[26]

The VHI proposal was turned down.

The VHI continued—unsuccessfully—to make the case that it should be allowed to become involved in providing new private hospitals. In a newsletter to members in 1986, for instance, the VHI argued that the payment of claims by itself would enable foreign-based companies to meet the capital costs of new hospitals while taking the profits out of the country. 'When it is clear that either additional or replacement private hospital facilities are required, the Board is of the opinion that, in the interest of its members, it should become directly involved in the provision and ownership of such facilities on a not-for-profit basis.'[27]

In more recent times, the strategic position of Vhi Healthcare on becoming involved in the provider market has changed. According to the current Chief Executive, Vincent Sheridan, 'unless there was a potential shortage of private bed capacity in the market—which appears to be extremely unlikely—then it is better that the role of the provider and purchaser of private facilities be separated. Vhi Healthcare would find itself in a difficult conflict of interest position if it were to be the main purchaser of private capacity and at the same time to be a provider competing for this business.'

By the end of 1986, three new private hospitals had come on stream. The Galvia in Galway (which replaced the older Calvary Private Hospital) fitted into the VHI's existing schemes B and C. However, bed charges for Blackrock Clinic (which opened for out-patients in 1984 and for in-patients in 1986) and the Mater Private (which replaced the Mater Nursing Home) were higher than for existing hospitals. In 1986, the Minister for Health, Barry Desmond TD, insisted that the VHI provide insurance cover for these hospitals. For this purpose the VHI created two extra plans, D and E. The VHI's most popular plan, B, would have covered only 45% of the cost of a semi-private room in the Mater Private and Blackrock Clinic and only 35% of private accommodation charges.

FINANCIAL CRISIS

A combination of continuing rises in costs and of restrictions on the VHI's freedom to raise premiums brought the organisation to a point in the late 1980s at which strong corrective action had to be taken.

In the year to the end of February 1983, claims exceeded income for the first time. In a statement following the presentation of its 26th annual report for the year, the VHI stated that 'the financial results show a subscription income of £57.3m, but claims amounting to £59.5m, for the first time ever, exceeded income. When administration expenses are added to claims, an underwriting deficit of £7.4m is shown. The surplus of £1.8m for the year was due to the strong performance of investments. The General Reserve was reduced to the equivalent of 2.1 months claims, at current rates, to cushion the effect on subscriptions, of exceptionally high levels of increase in public hospital charges.'

Costs were rising because of advances in medical and surgical techniques, growing consumer expectations, growing membership and increases in life expectancy. In addition the government, worried at the escalating demands which the cost of public hospitals was making on the Exchequer, substantially increased charges for private and semi-private rooms in public hospitals. The charges rose by 100% in 1982, by 50% in 1983 and by 25% in 1984 (Taylor, 1997).

Moreover, the advent of modern private hospitals such as Blackrock Clinic and the Mater Private with a wide range of up-to-date technologies pushed costs upwards for the VHI.

But though costs were rising, the Board was not free to raise subscriptions to the level it considered necessary to meet them.

For instance, between August 1981 and January 1984 charges for semi-private and private accommodation in public hospitals increased by 369% or roughly eleven times the rate of inflation for the same period. But when the Board sought to increase subscriptions by 15.9% from 1 March 1984, only a lesser increase of 13.5% was sanctioned.

As Mr Tom Ryan, Chief Executive from 1983 to 1994, put it, 'price increases were refused and bed costs were going up all the time.'[28]

To control costs, the VHI now negotiated two measures: budgets for private hospitals and all-in fees for consultants. The implementation of Plans A, B and C in 1979 to provide full cover for hospital charges had increased costs and the new budgets brought a measure of control in this area.[29]

Consultants who agreed not to bill patients for more than the amount covered by the VHI were known as 'participating consultants'. The list of participating consultants was given to GPs who could advise patients who would provide full cover and who would not. Before long, the vast majority of consultants were accepting VHI payment in full reimbursement for their services.[30]

Despite these measures, the VHI was heading into financial trouble. The year to the end of February 1988 brought a deficit of £12.3 million compared to a surplus of £2.9 million the previous year. The underwriting deficit was £23.7 million.

In response, the Minister for Health, Dr Rory O'Hanlon TD, commissioned a study on the future of the VHI from Mr Noel Fox of Oliver Freaney & Co. in 1988. He was then appointed to the post of Recovery Manager and became a member of the Board. Mr Fox, an insolvency and reconstruction expert, was familiar with health service funding issues. He had been engaged in a project on cost containment in the major teaching hospitals and was a member of the Commission on Health Funding.

'The VHI did not have the facility to raise cash from shareholders and it did not appear to have the facility to get government funding,' Mr Fox recalled later. With the reserves under threat, action needed to be taken quickly. In health insurance, rises in costs incurred by members are reflected very quickly in claims made on the insurer. Similarly, reductions in costs are reflected quickly in lower claims.[31]

Steps needed to secure the future of the VHI included subscription increases, benefit reductions and a new agreement with private hospitals.

The out-patient scheme to reimburse the cost of prescribed medicines was identified as a major drain on resources. It was an optional scheme which had been taken up by one third of the members. As might be expected, the members who took it up were those with greatest need for prescribed medicines (Ryan, 2006).[32] The scheme was discontinued. Administrative costs were reduced by an agreement with the private hospitals whereby they would accept reimbursement directly from the VHI, instead of being paid by the patient who would then make a claim on his or her health insurance. The private hospitals also agreed to an 18-month price freeze.

Needless to say, some of the cost-cutting measures, particularly the loss of the out-patient scheme, were unpopular with the public. 'For three to four years it was a nightmare,' recalled Ms Maureen Caulfield who became personnel manager in 1993. 'You did not want to admit you worked in VHI when at social occasions.'[33]

But the corrective measures worked. By the end of February 1990, the underwriting deficit had been eliminated and a small surplus of £0.7 million was recorded. In the following years, the Board began to restore the reserves.

These changes were achieved with Mr Fox and the existing Board and management (the latter led by Mr Tom Ryan, the Chief Executive of the VHI) working together with a degree of harmony and of success which may well be unusual in such situations. The team included a newcomer, Ms Maureen Lynott, who had been appointed Assistant General Manager, Market Development, in 1988 and who later went on to undertake a wide variety of managerial and consultancy roles in the health services.

On his arrival in the VHI, Mr Fox said later, he identified, as a key strength of the organisation, 'a loyal, committed, enthusiastic staff who wanted to adopt a forward-looking approach.' These values, he said, carried the recovery plan through.[34]

'I thought we did a pretty good job in the recovery,' the then chairman Mr Desmond Cashell said later. 'We also had an excellent CEO in Tom Ryan.'[35]

The major planks in the recovery, he recalled, were the removal of the out-patient scheme and of cover for maternity risks.[36]

In 1992 the government boosted its own revenues by taking £3 million from the VHI under powers included in the Finance Act of that year—a perverse compliment to the recovery programme perhaps!

In the following year, the Department of Health announced that it would move towards charging the VHI the 'full economic rate' for private beds in public hospitals—in other words the full cost of making public facilities, such as equipment, available to private patients in public hospitals would be recouped from these patients or their insurers. This policy has since been under gradual implementation.

A NEW ERA FOR PRIVATE HOSPITALS

As the 20th century drew to a close, the withdrawal of religious orders from the provision of private hospitals—due to falling vocations—was well advanced. Consequently, the sector was an increasingly commercial one and this brought with it increasing costs for Vhi Healthcare.

Half the country's private and semi-private beds were in private hospitals and half in public hospitals with 2,500 beds in each sector.[37]

In the new century, tax incentives to encourage the building of more private hospitals were introduced in the 2001 Finance Bill. Introducing the measure, the Minister for Finance, Mr McCreevy, argued that 'the benefit, in terms of additional beds, will be captured for the public health system as the Minister for Health and Children will designate a similar number of beds in public hospitals, as public beds, which prior to the provision of the new beds in the private hospital, had been designated as private. The effect of this measure will be to reduce the pressure on public hospital beds.'

Vhi Healthcare commissioned a capacity review study (2002) by PricewaterhouseCoopers to ensure that the benefits provided under the company's plans could still be provided, taking a five-year perspective. The study concluded that the already-existing capacity would meet projected demands over the period.

Vhi Healthcare subsequently criticised the incentives to provide more private hospitals. 'The creation of surplus private bed capacity would constitute a major driver of the cost of medical insurance,' wrote the Chief Executive Officer, Mr Vincent Sheridan, in the Annual Report for 2003. 'The dynamics of competition in the health market are different to those in other markets mainly because the level of demand is potentially inexhaustible. This is an important point, which is often overlooked.'

By then (2003), Vhi Healthcare already had agreements for cover with 34 private hospitals.

In his statement in the Annual Report for 2006, the Chairman, Mr Bernard Collins, described the increase in private bed capacity as 'unprecedented' and 'the single biggest challenge facing private health care in Ireland'.

This increase had been encouraged by generous tax reliefs available for such investment, and he repeated the VHI's earlier questioning of the wisdom of these tax incentives. There did not appear to be any significant demand from the public sector to use these new facilities. The cost of financing the new capacity, he said, would place 'huge pressure' on Vhi Healthcare's objective of providing its members with quality healthcare at affordable prices.

The Chief Executive, Mr Vincent Sheridan, was again critical of the move in 2006. 'This new capacity far exceeds what is required on the private side and there is no evidence of any significant transfer of public demand into these facilities,' he wrote. 'VHI Healthcare has consistently argued against this tax relief scheme.' Mr Sheridan also stated that 'it is not at all clear how it is proposed to reduce pressure on public hospital beds without a defined mechanism to transfer public demand to the private sector. The National Treatment Purchase Fund is not such a mechanism.'

Responding to claims by developers that the VHI was standing in the way of the provision of more private hospitals because of its practice of not giving guarantees that their beds would be covered, Mr Sheridan wrote in the 2005 Annual Report that 'VHI Healthcare does not stand in the way of the development of new hospital capacity. We are not in the business, however, of using the subscriptions of our members to provide comfort for developers. We will only extend cover facilities to those that bring competitive prices to the market.'

INTRODUCTION OF COMPETITION

The health insurance market was opened to competition with the passing of the Health Insurance Act, 1994.

The Act reflected the policy of the government that the system of community rating should be retained. It obliged all health insurers entering the market to apply the principles of community rating, open enrolment, lifetime cover and a minimum scale of benefits. While Vhi Healthcare had applied the principle of community rating from the start, this was the first time it was enshrined in legislation.

There was a sense of confidence in Vhi Healthcare at the time that the organisation would compete successfully, its then Chairman, Mr Noel Hanlon, recalled later.[38] Mr Aidan Walsh, Acting Chief Executive for two years until December 1997,[39] also recalled that the VHI was confident of taking on competition. Mr Walsh had been retained on a consultancy basis to bring, as he put it later, 'a general business perspective' to the organisation as part of its general preparation for competition and for a more commercial environment.[40]

Community rating means that older and younger people pay the same premium for the same level of cover, not only regardless of age but also regardless of health status. These principle is underwritten by a risk equalisation scheme in which companies with a disproportionately high number of young, healthy

members make a transfer of funds to companies with a disproportionately high number of older, less healthy members.

Prior to the drafting of the 1994 legislation, the VHI had lobbied
the government on the need to retain community rating and to
underpin the system with risk equalisation. According to Tom
Ryan, Chief Executive until 1994,

> Our point regarding community rating was immediately taken
> up by government. We found a ready acceptance in the EEC as
> well.[41]

The first new entrant on the Irish market was BUPA Ireland
Limited which was established in 1996. Its first prospectus had to
be amended because of complaints that age-related cash
plans which it included were in conflict with the principle of
community rating.

Prior to the arrival of BUPA, the only other competition faced by
Vhi Healthcare had been occupational schemes such as those for
the Garda Síochána and for employees of the Electricity Supply
Board. Some members of these schemes were also members of the
VHI. Also on the market had been cash plans offered by insurance
companies which paid specific cash amounts if subscribers fell ill.
The cash plans did not attempt to cover maintenance or
treatment costs in hospitals and had little impact on the VHI itself.
An application by Private Patients Plan to enter the Irish market
had been rejected by the Department of Health in 1988. PPP
continued to express an interest until 1990 when it said it would
not enter the market if it was community-rated.

Competition was good for Vhi Healthcare. Mr Derry Hussey,
Chairman from 1997 to 2003, recalled that 'competition sharpened
VHI enormously'. Customer service improved, schemes expanded
and membership continued to grow.[42]

An extremely low cost/income ratio has always been a feature
of VHI operations and this is an essential part of the culture of the

organisation—to maximise the amount of premium income that is used to pay claims on behalf of members, according to Mr Vincent Sheridan, Chief Executive Officer of Vhi Healthcare. Prior to the arrival of competition in the market the VHI cost/income ratio was around 6.5%. Competition increased costs on marketing, customer service etc. However in 2005, the cost/income ratio was only 8.4%. This compares with approximately 17% for BUPA and a range of 15% to 23% for other non-life insurers in the Irish market, he said.

TECHNOLOGY

The continuous growth in membership prompted the VHI to computerise at an early stage relative to most Irish companies. In the early 1970s the then Chief Executive, Mr Brian Savage, arranged for spare capacity on the Aer Lingus computers to be used by the VHI. The organisation got its first mainframe computer in 1977. An online claims assessment system was introduced in 1979. The VHI organised the first Federation of Hospital Funds IT Seminar in 1992.

In 1993, the VHI set up computer links with all the major hospitals. Private hospitals were given access to a Patient Inquiry System which gave them access to limited membership details of patients. Computer links between hospitals and the VHI for invoicing purposes were also introduced.

With use of the internet growing rapidly, Vhi Healthcare launched its e-commerce strategy in 1999 in the belief that one third of its members would be internet users within two years.[43]

Online facilities for Vhi Healthcare's then 7,000 corporate group schemes were introduced in 2001. In 2001 also, the VHI's health portal, www.vhi.ie, was launched to provide customised lifestyle and health information to the general public and to VHI members.

Long before decentralisation became a government policy, Vhi Healthcare decided to open a customer call centre (now referred to as a customer contact centre) away from its Dublin head office, in Kilkenny, in 2000. This was to take advantage of a large quality workforce available in Kilkenny and to provide for head office expansion in a lower cost centre than Dublin. This initiative has proved an outstanding success. The contact centre and its manager, Maurice Whelan, have won many national and international awards. In addition, the Kilkenny office has expanded to cover many other head office functions including claims processing, technology development and mail handling as well as answering member queries.

The investment in technology continues at an ever-increasing pace. In 2005, a new policy administration system went live. This took two years to design and implement at a cost of approximately €30 million. In 2006 work began on a completely new claims system.

WHITE PAPER, 1999, AND THE HEALTH INSURANCE (AMENDMENT) ACT, 2001

A White Paper published by the government in 1999 promised the introduction of risk equalisation, the incorporation of Vhi Healthcare with full commercial freedom and an investment of up to €60 million by the State.

The White Paper was followed by new legislation, the Health Insurance (Amendment) Act, 2001, which made important provisions in relation to competition, commercial freedom and community rating. These included:

1. Removal of constraints on covering GP, dental, out-patient and other 'ancillary' health services.
2. Establishment of the Health Insurance Authority with the power to recommend the implementation of risk equalisation.
3. A three-year 'holiday' from risk equalisation for new insurers.

4. Provision for a 'late entry premium' which could be charged to persons taking out health insurance for the first time after the age of 35 or after a significant lapse in cover.
5. Persons aged 65 or over to be entitled to take out health insurance cover.
6. Health insurers to be allowed to reduce premiums for persons under the age of 23 in full-time education.

RISK EQUALISATION

Although risk equalisation was provided for by the Health Insurance Act, 1994, the legislation which opened the market to competition,[44] it was not implemented until 1 January 2006, nine years after the arrival of the first competitor into the market. In the meantime, the desirability of introducing risk equalisation was examined by a range of bodies. All concluded that community rating—in which members pay the same premium for specific levels of cover regardless of age or other risk factors—must be underpinned by a risk equalisation scheme. Such a scheme would see a transfer of funds from insurers with a disproportionately high number of young and healthy members to insurers with disproportionately high number of older, less healthy members.[45]

In the interval between the passing of the 1994 Act and the implementation of risk equalisation at the start of January 2006, Vhi Healthcare consistently warned that delays in implementing the scheme were putting its financial survival at risk. Meanwhile, BUPA Ireland opposed risk equalisation and made a complaint to the European Commission. In the Annual Report for 2003, VHI Chairman Mr Derry Hussey noted that the EU Commission had concluded that the Irish government's risk equalisation scheme was justified.

In his review of operations for the year ended February 2003, Chief Executive Vincent Sheridan wrote that 'VHI Healthcare paid out €89 out of every €100 in premium earned in 2002–2003. We estimate that our competitor pays out in claims less than half of what is earned in premium! It is this anomaly that risk equalisation would go some way to eliminate.'

'In the absence of risk equalisation,' VHI Chairman Bernard Collins warned in the Annual Report for 2004, 'in this competitive community-rated market there is nothing that the Board or management can do to guarantee the long-term viability of this business.'

In December 2005, the Minister for Health and Children, Mary Harney TD, announced that she had decided to accept a recommendation from the Health Insurance Authority that risk equalisation be commenced. Risk equalisation would be in place from 1 January, she said.

The announcement came during a year in which Vhi Healthcare incurred a €32.3 million loss, largely because of the delays in introducing risk equalisation.

The loss of €32.3 million after-tax followed a surplus of €3.3 million the previous year. In his annual report, the Chairman Bernard Collins pointed out that this was the outcome of ten years of community-rated health insurance without risk equalisation.

That surplus of €3.3 million for the year to the end of February 2005 contrasted sharply with a surplus of €62.3 million the previous year.

In 2004 the Board had implemented a policy of financing the cost of the absence of risk equalisation out of its own reserves. In other words, this cost would no longer be passed on to members. The losses generated by this move underlined the impossibility of maintaining community rating without risk equalisation. On the other hand, if Vhi Healthcare was to continue to pass on to members the costs incurred because of the absence of risk equalisation it would be in danger of pricing itself out of the market.[46]

The formula for calculating the funds to be transferred to Vhi Healthcare under the risk equalisation scheme did not fully

compensate Vhi Healthcare for the cost of insuring a dispropor-
tionate number of older members, according to the Chairman,
Mr Bernard Collins. Nevertheless, the Minister's announcement
was welcome.[47]

However, the move was immediately challenged in the Irish
courts by BUPA Ireland. BUPA Ireland also initiated a challenge in
the European Court of First Instance on the issue.

On 23 November 2006, the High Court upheld the government's
decision to trigger the risk equalisation scheme. In delivering his
judgment, Mr Justice Liam McKechnie stated, 'I am satisfied that
community rating, open enrolment and lifetime cover, could not
operate in this country, in economically acceptable conditions,
without the presence of a risk equalisation scheme.'

He also stated: 'Risk equalisation is solely concerned with
equalising differences in risk profiles and uses age, gender and the
utilisation of bed nights as proxies in this regard. It does not in
any way reward failure or inefficiency and the size of transfers are
not driven by this factor. Moreover the scheme as established will
encourage the greatest possible competition in all areas other than
risk profile . . . The scheme is therefore absolutely necessary given
our system. Moreover it is fair, reasonable and proportionate.'

Following this decision, BUPA announced on 14 December 2006
that it was leaving the Irish market. The company subsequently
announced that it would appeal the High Court verdict but that
this appeal would not affect its decision to leave the market. In
2007, the Quinn Group purchased BUPA Ireland Ltd. In February
2007 the three-year 'holiday' from risk equalisation payments for
new entrants to the market was abolished by the Health Insurance
(Amendment) Act, 2007.

COMMERCIAL FREEDOM AND CHANGES IN CORPORATE STATUS
The status of Vhi Healthcare and the legislation which governed it
placed limits both on the organisation's ability to diversify its

products and on its freedom to implement price increases. An example of the former was a decision by the Department of Health in 1988 that a plan for a VHI scheme to cover the cost of GP treatment should not go ahead. As Mr Brian Dennis, chairman for the five years to 1987, put it:

> For any significant decision which we made we had to get permission from the Department of Health which I found very restraining.[48]

The 1999 White Paper had recognised the undesirability of this situation and had promised change:

> The environment in which VHI now operates is radically different from that which existed at the time of its establishment over 40 years ago. A change in the VHI's reporting relationship with government would reflect the change to the competitive market. The government consider that there is no longer any case for VHI to retain a direct link to the Department of Health and Children. They are satisfied that VHI's future lies in being regarded as an insurance business operating in accordance with a strong commercial and competitive mandate.[49]

In an announcement by the Minister for Health and Children on 25 April 2007, the government stated that it had decided on a number of measures concerning Vhi Healthcare. These included:

- Vhi Healthcare should become a conventional insurer authorised by the Financial Regulator by the end of 2008. The derogation from solvency requirements which the company had enjoyed would cease at that point.
- The immediate publication of a VHI Bill which, on enactment, would allow Vhi Healthcare to establish subsidiaries to operate its ancillary activities such as travel insurance and the Swiftcare

clinics. This measure would also remove the remaining powers of the Minister in relation to product development, pricing, etc.
• Risk equalisation payments would be discounted by 20%. Legislation to give effect to this latter change was passed by the Dáil on 26 April 2007.

Responding to the announcement, Vhi Healthcare warned that the existing formula for risk equalisation 'is already extremely weak'. A further dilution of risk equalisation, it said, would increase the profits of insurers with low risk profiles 'without any requirement for them to generate increased efficiency in their own operations or in the delivery of healthcare'.

On the removal of derogation from normal solvency requirements by the end of 2008, it stated that plans had already been in place to remove derogation by 2012 in accordance with an earlier decision by the Minister. The announcement of the earlier date 'has serious implications, not least for the continuation of the "not for profit" ethos of Vhi Healthcare. In addition, the dilution of the risk equalisation formula runs totally counter to the intention to remove derogation and may well render it impossible.'

Following a meeting with the Minister on 26 April, Vhi Healthcare said that the Health Insurance Authority had, in February 2007, 'noted that the current system [of risk equalisation] already provides significant financial advantage to insurers with low risk profiles'.

On the solvency requirements, it said it would work with an interdepartmental group led by the Department of Health and Children and the Department of Finance which was being set up to examine how the 2008 target might best be achieved.

PRODUCT DEVELOPMENT
The new century began with the enrolment of Vhi Healthcare's 1.5-millionth member in October 2000. The market had matured to a point at which the potential for adding extra members was

quite limited. By 2006, when membership stood at 1.55 million, the VHI had a market share of 76%. In these circumstances, the most promising opportunities for expansion lay in marketing a wide range of products both to existing members and to the public generally. By now, for basic health insurance, competition in the marketplace focused on corporate group schemes for younger people.

Because of the perceived maturity of the health insurance market, Vhi Healthcare therefore had to look outside the provision of purely health insurance products and services to ensure continued dynamism and growth. Diversification thus became an important strategic objective in the first years of the new century. The principal focus will always remain on health insurance and all diversification activities must provide added value to insured members and the community at large, Mr Vincent Sheridan, Chief Executive Officer of Vhi Healthcare, told the author.

Examples of the products and services currently offered by VHI Healthcare include:

VHI Healthcare Plans A–E and A–E Options: Hospital plans providing members with comprehensive cover for hospitals throughout Ireland, access to over 1,800 consultants, maternity benefits and other benefits.

HealthSteps from VHI Healthcare: A product providing cover for day-to-day medical costs.

LifeStage Choices from VHI Healthcare: A new approach to private health insurance offering plans tailored to suit the individual and their families as they progress through life.

MultiTrip from VHI Healthcare: An annual multi-trip travel insurance product which revolutionised the market, reducing prices substantially. Launched in February 2004, VHI Healthcare MultiTrip has quickly been established as market leader of the multi-trip travel insurance sector with an estimated 35% market share in this area and 300,000 policyholders.

Global from VHI *Healthcare:* A health insurance product for Irish residents moving or living abroad for more than six months, providing care should the member or their family fall ill.

Assist from VHI *Healthcare:* A standard service with VHI Healthcare hospital plans offering a 24-hour medical emergency helpline for members on holiday abroad, medical cover and a range of additional services.

VHI *Corporate Solutions:* A specialist team providing services on a range of employee health and wellbeing issues to corporate clients.

VHI *DeCare Dental:* Ireland's only dental insurance plan offering benefits to cover members' oral care needs.

www.vhi.ie: One of Ireland's most comprehensive healthcare websites.

VHI *HealthShop:* An online shop selling a range of health-related and cosmetic products.

NurseLine 24/7: A service offering access to a qualified nurse by phone 24 hours a day, 365 days a year.

BabyTalk from VHI *Healthcare:* A maternity helpline staffed by qualified midwives, providing a service to new and expectant mothers.

VHI *SwiftCare Clinics:* Ireland's first walk-in urgent care centres for people needing treatment for unexpected injuries and illnesses that do not pose a serious danger to a person's health such as sprains, bumps and bruises, cuts that may need a stitch and minor burns.

HEALTH PROMOTION

In line with trends in the health services generally Vhi Healthcare, at the start of the new century, re-positioned its brand to focus on wellness and on healthy living and not only on treatment for injuries or ill health. Examples included its Zest for Life campaign promoting healthy eating, stress management and exercise and Water for Life which promoted the benefits of drinking water.[50]

THE FIRST 50 YEARS ENDS ON THE BRINK OF CHANGE

By the end of its first 40 years, and following a decade of competition, Vhi Healthcare had a record 1.57 million members, 75% of the health insurance market, and reported a surplus of €70.3 million, although in excess of 50% of this surplus was an exceptional item, i.e. the release of part of a provision for future losses (the unexpired risk reserve). Risk equalisation had been introduced, though payments had not yet commenced, and a change in corporate status giving the organisation greater commercial freedom was imminent. It had substantially broadened its range of products. The business could also boast that, with an operating cost ratio of only 8.1%, it was far and away the most efficient insurer in the market.

During the year to the end of February 2007, Vhi Healthcare had agreements with well over 100 medical facilities of which 40 were private hospitals. It also entered into a new two-year agreement with 99% of hospital consultants for full coverage of their fees. Day care claims now accounted for almost 70% of all claims. This compared with 38% in 1996.

By the end of February 2007, Vhi Healthcare was employing 986 persons or 909 full-time equivalents spread across eight locations throughout Ireland. The organisation boasted a staff retention rate in excess of 95%.

The context in which Vhi Healthcare now operated was utterly different to that in which it had been established in 1957. Economic hardship had been replaced by prosperity. Irish people could afford to make new lifestyle choices. There had been, as Dr Bernadette Carr, Medical Director, Vhi Healthcare put it, 'a sea change regarding what people expect' and this meant, in turn, that people would have increasingly higher expectations in the area of health services. This presented a challenge and an opportunity for health insurers.[51]

One of the most significant changes in the delivery of health-care over the past 50 years has been the transfer of procedures from in-patient to day care and sideroom settings. In the 10 years from 1997 to 2007, the volume of claims paid for by Vhi Healthcare increased by 70% but in the same period the volume of in-patient claims fell by 6%, while the number of day care claims increased by 165%. Moreover, in the same period there was a 3% reduction in the average length of in-patient stay. This revolution in the delivery of healthcare, which Vhi Healthcare has encouraged and to an extent has demanded, is often overlooked when commentators review the development of bed capacity in Ireland over the past 20 years and has led to a huge productivity per bed, according to Mr Vincent Sheridan, Chief Executive Officer, Vhi Healthcare.

Other major challenges were outlined by Mr Sheridan, in his operations review in the 2007 Annual Report:

- To achieve a more equitable risk equalisation mechanism.
- To achieve the removal of derogation from solvency by 2008 without any follow-on threat to the cost of private health insurance.
- To meet the challenge of increased competition in the market.

Vhi Healthcare faced these and other challenges with confidence.

AFTERWORD:
A GLIMPSE OF THE FUTURE?

INTRODUCTION

Looking into the future, while tempting, is often a foolhardy enterprise. But with the health service experiencing a period of change in a newly-confident economy and in a new century the temptation, foolhardy or not, is difficult to resist.

This chapter attempts to look no more than two to five years ahead at a selection of possible developments in public and private healthcare and at two major health challenges—the ageing of the population and the rise in obesity—which seem to characterise the present era.

CONFIGURATION OF PUBLIC HOSPITALS

If one was to take a cue from the Hanly Report,[1] the 2001 health strategy[2] and other official documents published in recent years, one would say that the number of acute general hospitals in the country will be considerably reduced in the medium term. Instead, a relatively small number of big regional hospitals would provide a comprehensive, well-resourced service to larger catchment areas than at present. They would provide these services on their own sites and through out-patient clinics at those smaller hospitals which would have ceased to be acute hospitals. Some general acute hospitals would continue to work in remote areas.

While the Department of Health and Children, the Health Service Executive and a very large body of expert opinion might wish to see the hospital system move in this direction, the fact remains that developments of this sort have been recommended by bodies going back to the Hospitals Commission Report[3] of 1936; but political considerations based on local objections have made them impossible to implement. In the medium term, therefore, it is difficult to see the present configuration of public hospitals changing substantially.

If current government policy is implemented, a far higher proportion of consultants will work only in the public hospitals to which they are attached and will not have an off-site private practice. Patients will be more likely to be seen by a consultant than is the case today, as the move towards a consultant-provided service continues. Nurses will increasingly specialise and certain grades of nurses will be authorised to prescribe medicines.

PRIMARY CARE

If the Health Service Executive presses ahead with its plan to establish 500 primary care teams based on the recommendations of the 2001 *Primary Care Strategy*,[4] this area will be transformed. The single-handed GP, or the small practice with a couple of doctors and a practice nurse, will increasingly become a thing of the past. Primary care services will be provided by teams made up of doctors, nurses, physiotherapists, home helps and other health workers based in the same premises. The GPs in these teams will be resourced and equipped to provide a wider range of diagnostic and medical services so as to reduce the number of referrals to the acute hospital A&E departments. An increasing proportion of GPs will be women. Even if the provision of community care teams or primary care teams is implemented more slowly than expected and even if the target of 500 teams is never reached, the era of the single-handed GP appears to be coming to an end. Increasingly GPs will work with other GPs, through primary care teams, GP co-ops or group practices. The public may also find that, increasingly, GPs will drop their walk-in surgeries in favour of an appointments system to enable them to cope with demand.

AGEING OF THE POPULATION

The proportion of health spending devoted to services for older people will increase as the population ages. Approximately 11% of the population currently is over 65 and this is expected to rise to 15% in 2020. Medical technology will be one driver of increasing costs in the provision of health services for old people.[5]

Labour-intensive care will be another. In a statement following the announcement of the public spending estimates for 2007, the Minister for Health and Children, Mary Harney TD, indicated the sort of services the government intended to increase in the short term. She stated that 2007 would see the 'largest expansion in services for older people' and that these would include home care packages, extra home help hours, increased nursing home subventions and greater spending on palliative care.[6]

OBESITY

By 2006 and following more than ten years of prosperity, a new public health issue, which seems likely to preoccupy health planners in the near future, had emerged—obesity.

The report of the National Task Force on Obesity, *Obesity—the policy challenges*, published in 2005, outlined the scale of the problem.[7] Thirty-nine per cent of Irish adults were overweight and 18% were obese, it said:

> This year about 2,000 premature deaths in Ireland will be attributed to obesity and the numbers are growing relentlessly. Diseases which proportionally more obese people suffer from than the general population include hypertension, type 2 diabetes, angina, heart attack and osteoarthritis

The report suggests that the solution is likely to include public health as well as other measures and it calls for 'a fundamental examination of existing agricultural, industrial, economic and other policies and a determination to change them if they do not enable people to eat healthily and partake in physical activity.'

From the above, it seems likely that tackling obesity will be a long-term rather than a short-term issue. It will be a major health issue both in terms of treatment of diseases arising from obesity and in terms of preventive measures for the near to medium-term future.

PRIVATE HEALTHCARE AND PRIVATE INSURANCE

The next few years are likely to see more development in the area of private healthcare, especially private hospital care, than at any time in the past.

This is particularly due to tax incentives for the building of private hospitals and the current government policy of encouraging the development of private hospitals on the campus of public hospitals.

It seems likely that the new private hospitals will, in many instances, appoint their own consultants who will work exclusively for them. This development will be driven by the policy aim of the Department of Health and Children and the HSE to introduce public-only contracts for future consultants paid by the State.

Thus the distinction between public and private hospitals will be sharpened in terms of their workforces. That said, though, the private sector may find itself reliant on the State for a significant part of its income. This will be so if the National Treatment Purchase Fund continues as a mechanism for reducing public waiting lists by buying private treatment for patients.

Nevertheless, the major source of income for staffing and equipping the new hospitals will be payment for treating members of the VHI and other health insurers. Thus, it also seems likely that the advent of the new hospitals will bring about substantial increases in the cost of health insurance, especially given that the demand for hospital services tends to grow to meet the supply.

Following a High Court decision in 2006, however, it seems likely that the system of community rating, in which persons of all ages and levels of risk pay the same premium for the same level of cover, will continue, underpinned by risk equalisation payments.

It also seems likely that the development of primary care private facilities will continue to grow. The private urgent care walk-in clinics which the VHI has begun to open provide an example of such facilities. The clinics offer an alternative to attending a public hospital A&E department for minor injuries and they have so far been a success.

The mixture of public and private health has deep historical roots in Ireland and with more than half the population holding private health insurance this mixture can be expected to continue into the future.

CONCLUSION
The half century on which this book has focussed ended in a period of intense public debate on the administration and adequacy of health services. The regional health boards, which had been seen to represent an over-bureaucratisation of health administration, were replaced by the Health Service Executive. Will the HSE bring a new level of flexibility and focus to the provision of health services? Or will it come to be seen as a cumbersome monolith? Time will tell.

In general, and if current HSE policy is implemented, we can expect to see a greater focus on primary and community care than has ever been the case in the past. Whether this means that we will have fewer hospitals is another matter entirely. As mentioned elsewhere in this book and earlier in this chapter, public resistance to the closure of hospitals or to changes in their status is extremely strong.

Over a period of half a century enormous strides have been made in the health services, strides that are not always acknowledged. Eligibility for hospital services has been extended to the whole population, the older psychiatric institutions and county homes have all but disappeared, and expectations of the standard of care are higher than ever before.

These expectations alone, combined with the strongest economy the country has ever had, seem set to bring about a significant improvement in the health services in the near to medium future.

NOTES AND REFERENCES

Chapter 1. Overview and summary (PAGES 3–36)

1. See Part Two, The VHI.
2. Curry, John, *Irish Social Services*, Institute of Public Administration, Dublin, 2003.
3. *Report of the Commission on Health Funding*, Department of Health, Dublin, 1989.
4. *Value for Money Audit of the Irish Health System, Main Report*, Deloitte & Touche in conjunction with the York Health Economics Consortium, Department of Health and Children, Dublin, 2001.
5. Wiley, Miriam, 'Financing the Irish Health Services', in *Reflections on Health, Commemorating Fifty Years of the Department of Health 1947–1997*, Robins, J. (ed.), Department of Health, Dublin, 1997.
6. *RTE News*, 1 November 2006.
7. *RTE 1, Prime Time*, 15 September 2005.
8. *Leas Cross Report*, Health Service Executive, Dublin, 2006.
9. Mr Tom Ryan in an interview with the author, 2006.
10. Mr Derry Hussey in an interview with the author, 2006.
11. Health Insurance Act, 1994, Section 12.

Chapter 2. Hospitals—expansion, contraction and resistance (PAGES 37–48)

1. Barrington, Ruth, *Health Medicine & Politics in Ireland 1900–1970*, Institute of Public Administration, Dublin, 1987.
2. Curry, John, *Irish Social Services*, Institute of Public Administration, Dublin, 2003.
3. Hensey, Brendan, *The Health Services of Ireland*, Institute of Public Administration, Dublin, 1979.
4. See Chapter 8.
5. See Chapter 8.
6. The Hospitals Commission, *First General Report*, Stationery Office, Dublin, 1936.
7. *Outline of the Future Hospital System, Report of the Consultative Council on the General Hospital Service*, Stationery Office, Dublin, 1968.
8. *The Health Services and their Further Development*, Stationery Office, Dublin, 1966.

9. Curry, *ibid*.
10. Curry, *ibid*.
11. Curry (2003) notes that a similar commitment had been made seven years earlier in a previous strategy, *Shaping a Healthier Future* (1994).
12. See Chapter 8.
13. See Chapter 6.
14. *Audit of Structures and Functions in the Health System*, Prospectus Management Consultants, Stationery Office, Dublin, 2003.
15. *Report of the National Task Force on Medical Staffing (Hanly Report)*, Stationery Office, Dublin, 2003.
16. 'Dublin hospitals at risk from EU directive', *The Irish Times*, 1 November 2005.
17. *Finance Bill, 2001*, Stationery Office, Dublin.
18. *Tánaiste announces plan for 1,000 new public hospital beds over 5 years*, Department of Health and Children Press Release, 14 July 2005.
19. *Tánaiste determined that private and public healthcare can work together*, Progressive Democrats Press Release, 5 April 2006.

Chapter 3. Care in the community—community care and primary care
(PAGES 49–65)

1. The term 'community care' as used in this chapter encompasses primary care, measures to control infectious diseases and services provided by voluntary and community groups. 'Primary care' encompasses personal services provided by salaried professionals such as doctors, public health nurses, physiotherapists etc. to persons who are not hospital in-patients.
2. Curry, John, *Irish Social Services*, Institute of Public Administration, Dublin, 2003.
3. *The Health Services and their Further Development*, Stationery Office, Dublin, 1966.
4. Boland, Michael, 'The Role of General Practice in a Developing Health Service', in *Reflections on Health, Commemorating Fifty Years of the Department of Health 1947–1997*, Robins, J. (ed.), Department of Health, Dublin, 1997.
5. Barrington, Ruth, *Health, Medicine & Politics in Ireland 1900–1970*, Institute of Public Administration, Dublin, 1987.
6. *The Future Organisation of General Practice in Ireland: A Discussion Document*, Irish College of General Practitioners, Dublin, 1986.
7. Boland, *ibid*.
8. Mangan, Ita, *The Medical Card—Affording Health on a Low Income*, Comhairle, Dublin, 2004.
9. *Primary Care: A New Direction*, Department of Health and Children, Dublin, 2001.
10. 'HSE to roll out 500 primary care teams', *Irish Medical News*, 31 October 2006.

11. See Part Two, The VHI.
12. Coakley, Davis, 'Out of the Shadow—Developing Services for the Elderly', in *Reflections on Health, Commemorating Fifty Years of the Department of Health 1947–1997*, Robins, J. (ed.), Department of Health, Dublin, 1997.
13. *Care of the Aged*, Stationery Office, Dublin, 1968.
14. *The Years Ahead: Policy for the Elderly*, Stationery Office, Dublin, 1988.
15. *The Years Ahead Report: A Review of the Implementation of its Recommendations*, National Council on Ageing and Older People, Dublin, 1997.
16. The National Council on Ageing and Older People, recommended by the 1968 report, was established in 1981 under the name National Council for the Aged.
17. Website of Carers Association, *http://www.carersireland.com*, 2006.
18. Barrington, *ibid*.
19. Hensey, Brendan, *The Health Services of Ireland*, Institute of Public Administration, Dublin, 1972.
20. *http://www.imb.ie*, 2006.
21. O'Morain, Padraig, *The Irish Association of Directors of Nursing and Midwifery, 1904–2004*, IADNAM, Dublin, 2004.
22. *District Nursing Service* (circular 27/66), Department of Health, Dublin, 1966.

Chapter 4. Mental health care—from the institution to the community
(PAGES 66–79)

1. Walsh, Dermot, 'Mental Health Care in Ireland 1945–1997 and the Future', in *Reflections on Health, Commemorating Fifty Years of the Department of Health 1947–1997*, Robins, J. (ed.), Department of Health, Dublin, 1997.
2. Hensey, Brendan, *The Health Services of Ireland*, Institute of Public Administration, Dublin, 1979.
3. Ferriter, Diarmaid, *The Transformation of Ireland 1900–2000*, Profile Books, London, 2004.
4. Malcolm, Elizabeth, 'The house of strident shadows: The asylum, the family and emigration in post-Famine rural Ireland', in *Medicine, Disease and the State in Ireland, 1650–1940*, Jones, G., and Malcolm, E. (eds), Cork University Press, Cork, 1999.
5. *Report of the Commission of Inquiry on Mental Illness*, Stationery Office, Dublin, 1966.
6. Curry, John, *Irish Social Services*, Institute of Public Administration, Dublin, 2003.
7. *Quality and Fairness, A Health System for You*, Stationery Office, Dublin, 2001.
8. Walsh, *ibid*.
9. *Green Paper on Mental Health*, Stationery Office, Dublin, 1992.
10. *White Paper on Mental Health*, Stationery Office, Dublin, 1995.

11. Website of the Mental Health Commission, *http://www.mhcirl.ie/*, 2006.
12. Website of the Mental Health Commission, *http://www.mhcirl.ie/*, 2006.
13. Ferriter, *ibid.*
14. *Mental Health Commission Annual Report 2004, including the Report of the Inspector of Mental Health Services*, Mental Health Commission, Dublin, 2005.
15. Address by Micheál Martin, TD, Minister for Health and Children on the occasion of his visit to the Central Mental Hospital, 19 February 2003.
16. *Forensic Mental Health Services for Adults in Ireland, Discussion Paper*, Mental Health Commission, Dublin, 2006.

Chapter 5. The health services and disability (PAGES 80–92)
1. *Quality and Fairness, A Health System for You*, Stationery Office, Dublin, 2001.
2. Website of Rehab, *http://www.rehab.ie*, 2006.
3. See Chapter 4.
4. Ryan, Annie, *Walls of Silence*, Red Lion Press, Kilkenny, 1999.
5. Pre-Budget Submission, 2005, National Disability Authority.
6. Curry, John, *Irish Social Services*, Institute of Public Administration, Dublin, 2003.
7. Colgan, Anne, 'People with Disabilities and the Health Services', in *Reflections on Health, Commemorating Fifty Years of the Department of Health 1947–1997*, Robins, J. (ed.), Department of Health, Dublin, 1997.
8. The present author, when covering disability issues for *The Irish Times* in the late 80s and early 90s was struck by the fact that he had never once heard a disabled person or a relative of a disabled person say that the health board had been helpful in any matter.
9. *Training and Employing the Handicapped, Report of a Working Party Established by the Minister for Health*, Stationery Office, Dublin, 1975.
10. *Towards an Independent Future, Report of the Review Group on Health and Personal Social Services for People with Physical and Sensory Disabilities*, Stationery Office, Dublin, 1996.
11. Hensey, Brendan, *The Health Services of Ireland*, Institute of Public Administration, Dublin, 1979.
12. Colgan, *ibid.*
13. Commission on the Status of People with Disabilities, *A Strategy for Equality*, Department for Equality and Law Reform, Dublin, 1996.
14. Website of the Department of Justice, Equality and Law Reform, *http://www.justice.ie*, 2006.
15. Pre-Budget Submission, 2006, People with Disabilities in Ireland.
16. *Health Sectoral Plan Sets Out Clear Commencement Dates for New Disability Entitlements*, Department of Health and Children Press Release, 21 July 2006.

17. Lawlor, Rita, *Moving On*, Marino, Dublin, 1999.
18. *NPSDDC Annual Report 2005*, Health Research Board, Dublin, 2006.
19. Pre-Budget Submission, 2006, People with Disabilities in Ireland.

Chapter 6. From county council to Health Service Executive (PAGES 93–108)
1. Ferriter, Diarmaid, *The Transformation of Ireland 1900–2000*, Profile Books, London, 2004.
2. Curry, John, *Irish Social Services*, Institute of Public Administration, Dublin, 2003.
3. Hensey, Brendan, *The Health Services of Ireland*, Institute of Public Administration, Dublin, 1979.
4. Ferriter (2004) notes that the Free State government was keeping files comparing the social and economic status of the people of Northern Ireland and the South.
5. *White Paper: Outline of Proposals for the Improvement of the Health Services*, Stationery Office, Dublin, 1947.
6. O'Dwyer, Jerry, 'Strategic Planning in the Irish Health Services', in R*eflections on Health, Commemorating Fifty Years of the Department of Health 1947–1997*, Robins, J. (ed.), Department of Health, Dublin, 1997.
7. *White Paper: The Health Services and their Further Development*, Stationery Office, Dublin, 1966.
8. O'Dwyer, *ibid.*
9. *Report of the Commission of Inquiry on Mental Illness*, Stationery Office, Dublin, 1966.
10. Walsh, Dermot, 'Mental Healthcare in Ireland 1945–1997 and the Future', in *Reflections on Health, Commemorating Fifty Years of the Department of Health 1947–1997*, Robins, J. (ed.), Department of Health, Dublin, 1997.
11. Viney, Michael, *Growing old in Ireland, The Irish Times articles*, The Irish Times, Dublin, 1967.
12. See Chapter 8.
13. *Report of the Commission on Health Funding*, Department of Health, Dublin, 1989.
14. *The Psychiatric Services: Planning for the Future*, Stationery Office, Dublin, 1984.
15. *Shaping a Healthier Future*, Stationery Office, Dublin, 1994.
16. O'Dwyer, *ibid.*
17. *Quality and Fairness, A Health System for You*, Stationery Office, Dublin, 2001.
18. See Chapter 9.
19. Prospectus, *Audit of Structures and Functions in the Health System on behalf of the Department of Health and Children*, Stationery Office, Dublin, 2003.
20. *Tánaiste announces Board of the Interim Health Information and Quality Authority*, Department of Health and Children Press Release, 28 January 2005.

21. *Complaints Regulations under Part 9 of the Health Act 2004*, Department of Health and Children Press Release, 21 December 2006.

Chapter 7. The medical and nursing professions (PAGES 109–133)

1. Royal Commission on the Poor Laws and the Relief of Distress, *Report on Ireland*, 1909.
2. Deeny could not stand Browne's abrasiveness and left the Department of Health in 1950. He returned after Browne's downfall and was associated with the implementation of a new Mother and Child Scheme.
3. Speech to IMA, June 1946, Miscellaneous Memoranda, No. 3, Deeny Papers, RCSI, cited in Barrington, Ruth, *Health, Medicine & Politics in Ireland 1900–1970*, Institute of Public Administration, Dublin, 1987.
4. See Chapter 9.
5. Letter from the Taoiseach to Dr McQuaid, 9 April 1951, Cabinet files.
6. Journal of the Irish Medical Association, Vol. xlv, No. 270, Dec. 1959, p. 183.
7. Brown, Patricia, and Chadwick, Geoffrey, 'Management and the Health Professional', in *Reflections on Health, Commemorating Fifty Years of the Department of Health 1947–1997*, Robins, J. (ed.), Department of Health, Dublin, 1997.
8. Report of the Study Group on the General Medical Service, 12 February 1962, papers of Deeny, Dr J., Library of the Royal College of Surgeons in Ireland, referenced in Barrington (1987).
9. *Outline of the Future Hospital System, Report of the Consultative Council on the General Hospital Service*, Stationery Office, Dublin, 1968.
10. Brown and Chadwick, *ibid.*
11. O'Dowd, Tom, O'Kelly, Mark, O'Kelly, Fergus, *Structure of General Practice in Ireland, 1982–2005*. Presentation to the annual general meeting of the Irish College of General Practitioners, 2006, by Professor Tom O'Dowd.
12. Boland, Michael, *The Role of General Practice in a Developing Health Service* in *Reflections on Health, ibid.*
13. See Chapter 3.
14. 'HSE to roll out 500 primary care teams', *Irish Medical News*, 31 October 2006.
15. See Chapter 8.
16. Curry, John, *Irish Social Services*, Institute of Public Administration, Dublin, 2003.
17. Ferriter, Diarmaid, *The Transformation of Ireland 1900–2000*, Profile Books, London, 2004.
18. *Value for Money Audit of the Irish Health System, Main Report*, Deloitte & Touche in conjunction with the York Health Economics Consortium, Department of Health and Children, Dublin, 2001.
19. Brown and Chadwick, *ibid.*

20. Talks on contracts for consultants to resume this week', *The Irish Times*, 6 November 2006.
21. *Report of the Commission on Nursing, A blueprint for the future*, Stationery Office, Dublin, 1998.
22. 'Midwives in Ireland', paper by Miss Eileen Joy, matron of the Coombe Hospital, to a meeting of the Irish Matrons Association, 1912, in *Irish Association of Directors of Nursing and Midwifery, 1904–2004*, A History, O'Morain, P., IADNAM, Dublin, 2004.
23. See Chapter 3.
24. O'Morain, *ibid*.
25. McCarthy, Geraldine, 'Nursing and the Health Services', in *Reflections on Health, ibid*.
26. National Council for the Professional Development of Nursing and Midwifery website, *http://www.ncnm.ie*, 2006.

Chapter 8. Financing the health system (PAGES 134–149)

1. Hensey, Brendan, *The Health Services of Ireland*, Institute of Public Administration, Dublin, 1979.
2. Barrington, Ruth, *Health, Medicine & Politics in Ireland 1900–1970*, Institute of Public Administration, Dublin, 1987.
3. This figure, however, does not include private fees and thereby understates the true level of spending.
4. *White Paper: The Health Services and their Further Development*, Stationery Office, Dublin, 1966.
5. Boland, Michael, 'The Role of General Practice in a Developing Health Service', in *Reflections on Health, Commemorating Fifty Years of the Department of Health 1947–1997*, Robins, J. (ed.), Department of Health, Dublin, 1997.
6. Wiley, Miriam, 'Financing the Irish Health Services', in *Reflections on Health, ibid*.
7. Taylor, Desmond, *The Voluntary Health Insurance Board, the First Forty Years 1957–1997*, unpublished, 1997.
8. The source of this information in Taylor (1997) is Dr F.O.C. Meenan's *Historical and Social Portrait of St Vincent's Hospital*, published by Gill & Macmillan in 1995.
9. Curry, John, *Irish Social Services*, Institute of Public Administration, Dublin, 2003.
10. Deloitte & Touche, *Value for Money Audit of the Irish Health System*, Department of Health and Children, Dublin, 2001.
11. See Chapter 3.
12. *Report of the Commission on Health Funding*, Stationery Office, Dublin, 1989.

13. *White Paper: Private Health Insurance*, Department of Health and Children, Dublin, 1999.
14. *Report of the Commission on Health Funding, ibid.*
15. *Quality and Fairness, A Health System for You*, Department of Health and Children, Dublin, 2001.
16. Deloitte & Touche, *ibid.*
17. *Quality and Fairness, ibid.*
18. *Fall in waiting times, National Treatment Purchase Fund given new responsibilities*, Department of Health and Children Press Release, 4 May 2004.
19. National Treatment Purchase Fund, Patient Treatment Register, *http://www.ptr.ie/Pages/ptrHome.asp*, 2006.
20. Interestingly the Minister noted that the new casemix project involved developing links with the Australian system. The development of the private health insurance system introduced in 1957 was also based on the Australian model. Thus, Australia has had a considerable influence on the Irish healthcare system.
21. *Minister Martin launches a major modernisation and expansion of Casemix*, Department of Health and Children Press Release, 1 April 2004.
22. Wiley, *ibid.*
23. Purcell, Declan, *Presentation to FTC/DoJ Joint Hearing Competition Policy in the Irish Health Sector, Declan Purcell Member of the Irish Competition Authority, and Director of Advocacy*, 30 September 2003.

Chapter 9. Controversy and scandal (PAGES 150–162)
1. Mahon, Evelyn, 'The Development of a Health Policy for Women', in *Reflections on Health, Commemorating Fifty Years of the Department of Health 1947–1997*, Robins, J. (ed.), Department of Health, Dublin, 1997.
2. Ferriter, Diarmaid, *The Transformation of Ireland 1900–2000*, Profile Books, London, 2004.
3. Mahon, *ibid.*
4. Barrington, Ruth, *Health, Medicine & Politics in Ireland 1900–1970*, Institute of Public Administration, Dublin, 1987.
5. Farmar, Tony, *Holles Street 1894–1994*, A. & A. Farmar, Dublin, 1994.
6. The circumstances in which a couple could have sex during the safe period were those which the Pope called circumstances 'such as those which not rarely arise from medical, eugenic, economic and social so-called "indications"'. To use the safe period to have sex without conception in the absence of such circumstances was wrong. And if a couple could not have sexual intercourse because, for medical reasons, the woman must not become pregnant, then they must abstain from every type of sexual activity.

7. *Allocution of Pope Pius XII to midwives*, Vatican, 29 October 1951.
8. *Report of the Tribunal of Inquiry into the Infection with HIV and Hepatitis C of Persons with Haemophilia and Related Matters*, Department of Health and Children, 2002.
9. *Report of the Tribunal of Inquiry into the Blood Transfusion Service Board*, Department of Health and Children, Dublin, 1997.
10. *Report of Dr Deirdre Madden on Post Mortem Practice and Procedures*, Department of Health and Children, Dublin, 2006.
11. *The Lourdes Hospital Inquiry*, Stationery Office, Dublin, 2006.
12. *The Irish Times*, 17 November 2006.
13. *RTE News*, 1 November 2006.
14. *Trends in Staphylococcus aureus/MRSA bacteraemia in Ireland*, HPSC, Dublin, 2006.
15. *The Irish Times*, 17 May 2005.
16. *RTE 1, Prime Time*, 15 September 2005.
17. *Leas Cross Report*, Health Service Executive, Dublin, 2006.
18. The Northern Area Health Board was succeeded by the HSE (Northern Area) in 2005.
19. *The Irish Times*, 11 November 2006.
20. *The Irish Times, ibid.*
21. *The Irish Times*, 2 October 2003.
22. Farmar, Tony, *ibid.*
23. *The Irish Times*, 6 October 1999.
24. *Commission on Patient Safety and Quality Assurance has its inaugural meeting today*, Department of Health and Children Press Release, 26 January 2007.

Chapter 10. How the health of the population has changed (PAGES 163–172)

1. Kelleher, Cecily, 'Promoting Health', in *Reflections on Health, Commemorating Fifty Years of the Department of Health 1947–1997*, Robins, J. (ed.), Department of Health, Dublin, 1997.
2. Statement by Ambassador H.E. Mr Declan O'Donovan, Head of the Delegation of Ireland at the Second World Assembly on Ageing, Madrid, Spain, 11 April 2002. See website *http://www.un.org/ageing/coverage/irelandE.htm*, 2006.
3. *Census 2001*, Office for National Statistics, London, 2002.
4. Central Statistics Office website, *http://www.cso.ie/statistics/lifeexpect.htm*, 2007.
5. *Health: The Wider Dimensions*, Stationery Office, Dublin, 1986.
6. Health Education Bureau, *Promoting Health Through Public Policy*, Dublin, 1987.
7. *Shaping a Healthier Future*, Stationery Office, Dublin, 1994
8. *Quality and Fairness—a health system for you*, Stationery Office, Dublin, 2001.
9. Website of the HPSC, *http://www.hpsc.ie*, 2006.

10. *Martin announces total ban on smoking in the workplace*, Department of Health and Children Press Release, 30 January 2003.

11. Ferriter, Diarmaid, *The Transformation of Ireland 1900–2000*, Profile Books, London, 2004.

12. *Strategic Task Force on Alcohol, Interim Report*, Department of Health and Children, Dublin, 2002.

13. Corrigan, Desmond, *Facts about drug misuse in Ireland*, Health Promotion Unit, Department of Health and Children, Dublin, 2003.

14. AIDS *Strategy 2000*, Report of the National AIDS Strategy Committee, Department of Health and Children, Dublin, 2000.

15. AIDS *Strategy 2000, ibid.*

16. AIDS *Strategy 2000, ibid.*

17. AIDS *Strategy 2000, ibid.*

18. Website of BreastCheck, *http://www.breastcheck.ie*, 2006.

19. Devlin, John, 'The State of Health in Ireland', in *Reflections on Health, Commemorating Fifty Years of the Department of Health 1947–1997*, Robins, J. (ed.), Department of Health, Dublin, 1997.

Part Two: Vhi Healthcare (PAGES 175–214)

1. Ferriter, Diarmaid, *The Transformation of Ireland 1900–2000*, Profile Books, London, 2004.

2. *White Paper: Private Health Insurance*, Stationery Office, Dublin, 1999.

3. Taylor, Desmond, *The Voluntary Health Insurance Board, The First Forty Years 1957–1997*, VHI archives, 1997.

4. Mr Desmond Taylor joined the VHI on its inception in 1957 and became its personnel manager in 1972. This chapter draws heavily on his account, *The Voluntary Health Insurance Board, The First Forty Years 1957–1997*, now in the VHI archives. I am also grateful to those who so faithfully maintained archival material from 1957 to the present day.

5. Mr Michael Collins-Powell, first manager of the VHI's Cork office, in an interview with the author, 2006.

6. Mr Tom Ryan, Chief Executive, 1983–1994 in an interview with the author, 2006.

7. See Chapter 6.

8. See Chapter 10.

9. *Report of the Advisory Body on Voluntary Health Insurance Scheme*, Stationery Office, Dublin, 1956.

10. *Report of the Advisory Body on Voluntary Health Insurance Scheme, ibid.*

11. Dáil Éireann—Volume 160—7 November 1956—Voluntary Health Insurance Bill, 1956—Second Stage.

12. Mr Vincent Sheridan in an interview with the author, 2006.

13. Mr Bob Graham in an interview with the author, 2006.
14. Barrington, Ruth, *Health, Medicine & Politics in Ireland, 1900–1970*, Institute of Public Administration, Dublin, 1987.
15. Ms Maureen Caulfield, personnel manager, 1993–2005 in an interview with the author, 2006.
16. Mr McGloughlin's recollections are contained in his winning essay in a competition in memory of Mr Noel Burke and cited in Taylor, *ibid*. He retired as marketing manager in 1988.
17. Mr Bob Graham in an interview with the author, 2006.
18. Mr Leonard McGloughlin, who retired as marketing manager in 1988, in an interview with the author, 2006.
19. Mr Michael Collins-Powell, *ibid*.
20. By 2007 there were more than 8,000 group secretaries.
21. Mr Leonard McGloughlin, *ibid*.
22. Mr Brian Savage in an interview with the author, 2006.
23. *Address by Mr Charles J. Haughey, TD, Minister for Health and Social Welfare, at the official opening of the new public office of the Voluntary Health Insurance Board at 5.30 p.m. on Thursday 3 May 1979*, Department of Health Press Release, 3 May 1979.
24. Mr Tom Ryan, Chief Executive 1983–1994, in an interview with the author, 2006.
25. Central Statistics Office, Dublin, 2007.
26. Mr Brian Dennis, Chairman of the VHI 1982–1987, in an interview with the author, 2006.
27. *VHI News*, January 1986.
28. Mr Tom Ryan in an interview with the author, 2006.
29. Ms Maureen Caulfield, *ibid*.
30. According to Mr Noel Hanlon, Chairman 1992–1997, the implementation of a system of full cover was one of the most important developments in his period in office and was achieved after 'very difficult' negotiations. Interview with the author, 2006.
31. Mr Noel Fox in an interview with the author, 2006.
32. Mr Tom Ryan, *ibid*.
33. Ms Maureen Caulfield, *ibid*.
34. Mr Noel Fox, *ibid*.
35. Mr Desmond Cashell was Chairman from 1987 to 1992 and succeeded Mr Brian Dennis. He was succeeded in turn by Mr Noel Hanlon.
36. Mr Desmond Cashell in an interview with the author, 2006.
37. *White Paper: Private Health Insurance, ibid*.
38. Mr Noel Hanlon, Chairman 1992–1997, in an interview with the author, 2006.
39. Mr Walsh succeeded Mr Brian Duncan, Chief Executive 1995–1996.

40. Mr Aidan Walsh in an interview with the author, 2006.
41. Mr Tom Ryan, *ibid.*
42. Mr Derry Hussey in an interview with the author, 2006.
43. Mr Tattan was Chief Executive for two years up to December 2000. He was succeeded by Mr Vincent Sheridan, formerly of the Hibernian Group.
44. Health Insurance Act, 1994, Section 12.
45. Bodies which recommended or supported the introduction of risk equalisation included the Advisory Group on Risk Equalisation, established by the government in 1998, the Society of Actuaries in 2002, the Competition Authority in 2002, The York Health Insurance Consortium (commissioned by the Health Insurance Authority) in 2003 and FGS Consulting and DKM Economic Consultants in 2005.
46. Mr Vincent Sheridan in an interview with the author, 2006.
47. Mr Bernard Collins in an interview with the author, 2006
48. Mr Brian Dennis, *ibid.*
49. *White Paper: Private Health Insurance, ibid.*
50. 2002.
51. Dr Bernadette Carr, Medical Director, VHI, in an interview with the author, 2006.

Afterword (PAGES 215–220)

1. *Report of the National Task Force on Medical Staffing (Hanly Report)*, Stationery Office, Dublin, 2003.
2. *Quality and Fairness—a health system for you*, Stationery Office, Dublin, 2001.
3. The Hospitals Commission, *First General Report*, Stationery Office, Dublin, 1936.
4. *Primary Care: A New Direction*, Stationery Office, Dublin, 2001.
5. Barrett, Dr Alan, 'Can we afford our ageing population?' *The Irish Times*, 12 September 2006.
6. *New hospital units and older people high priorities in €14.5bn health funding 2007*, Department of Health and Children Press Release, 16 November 2006.
7. *Obesity—the Policy Challenges, The Report of the National Task Force on Obesity*, Stationery Office, Dublin, 2005.

BIBLIOGRAPHY

— AIDS *Strategy 2000, Report of the National* AIDS *Strategy Committee*, Stationery Office, Dublin, 2000.

— *Audit of Structures and Functions in the Health System*, Prospectus Management Consultants, Stationery Office, Dublin, 2003.

— Barrington, Ruth, *Health, Medicine & Politics in Ireland 1900–1970*, Institute of Public Administration, Dublin, 1987.

— Boland, Michael, 'The Role of General Practice in a Developing Health Service', in *Reflections on Health: Commemorating Fifty Years of the Department of Health 1947–1997*, Robins, J. (ed.), Department of Health, Dublin, 1997.

— Brown, Patricia, and Chadwick, Geoffrey, 'Management and the Health Professional', in *Reflections on Health: Commemorating Fifty Years of the Department of Health 1947–1997*, Robins, J. (ed.), Department of Health, Dublin, 1997.

— *Care of the Aged*, Stationery Office, Dublin, 1968.

— Coakley, Davis, 'Out of the Shadow––Developing Services for the Elderly', in *Reflections on Health: Commemorating Fifty Years of the Department of Health 1947–1997*, Robins, J. (ed.), Department of Health, Dublin, 1997.

— Colgan, Anne, 'People with Disabilities and the Health Services', in *Reflections on Health: Commemorating Fifty Years of the Department of Health 1947–1997*, Robins, J. (ed.), Department of Health, Dublin, 1997.

— Commission on the Status of People with Disabilities, *A Strategy for Equality*, Department for Equality and Law Reform, Dublin, 1996.

— Corrigan, Desmond, *Facts about drug misuse in Ireland*, Stationery Office, Dublin, 2003.
— Curry, John, *Irish Social Services*, Institute of Public Administration, Dublin, 2003.
— Devlin, John, 'The State of Health in Ireland', in *Reflections on Health: Commemorating Fifty Years of the Department of Health 1947–1997*, Robins, J. (ed.), Department of Health, Dublin, 1997.
— Farmar, Tony, *Holles Street 1894–1994*, A. & A. Farmar, Dublin, 1994.
— Ferriter, Diarmaid, *The Transformation of Ireland 1900–2000*, Profile Books, London, 2004.
— *Forensic Mental Health Services for Adults in Ireland*, Discussion Paper, Mental Health Commission, Dublin, 2006.
— *Green Paper on Mental Health*, Stationery Office, Dublin, 1992.
— *Health: The Wider Dimensions*, Stationery Office, Dublin, 1987.
— Hensey, Brendan, *The Health Services of Ireland*, Institute of Public Administration, Dublin, 1979.
— Kelleher, Cecily, 'Promoting Health', in *Reflections on Health: Commemorating Fifty Years of the Department of Health 1947–1997*, Robins, J. (ed.), Department of Health, Dublin, 1997.
— Lawlor, Rita, *Moving On*, Marino, Dublin, 1999.
— *Leas Cross Report*, Health Service Executive, Dublin, 2006.
— Mahon, Evelyn, 'The Development of a Health Policy for Women', in *Reflections on Health: Commemorating Fifty Years of the Department of Health 1947–1997*, Robins, J. (ed.), Department of Health, Dublin, 1997.
— Malcolm, Elizabeth, 'The house of strident shadows: The asylum, the family and emigration in post-Famine rural Ireland', in *Medicine, Disease and the State in Ireland, 1650–1940*, Jones, G., and Malcolm, E. (eds), Cork University Press, Cork, 1999.
— Mangan, Ita, *The Medical Card: Affording Health on a Low Income*, Comhairle, Dublin, 2004.

— McCarthy, Geraldine, 'Nursing and the Health Services', in *Reflections on Health: Commemorating Fifty Years of the Department of Health 1947–1997*, Robins, J. (ed.), Department of Health, Dublin, 1997.

— *Mental Health Commission Annual Report 2004, including the Report of the Inspector of Mental Health Services*, Mental Health Commission, Dublin, 2005.

— NPSDDC *Annual Report 2005*, Health Research Board, Dublin, 2006.

— *Obesity—the Policy Challenges: The Report of the National Task Force on Obesity*, Stationery Office, Dublin, 2005.

— O'Dwyer, Jerry, 'Strategic Planning in the Irish Health Services', in *Reflections on Health: Commemorating Fifty Years of the Department of Health 1947–1997*, Robins, J. (ed.), Department of Health, Dublin, 1997.

— O'Morain, Padraig, *The Irish Association of Directors of Nursing and Midwifery, 1904–2004*, IADNAM, Dublin, 2004.

— *Outline of the Future Hospital System: Report of the Consultative Council on the General Hospital Service*, Stationery Office, Dublin, 1968.

— *Primary Care: A New Direction*, Stationery Office, Dublin, 2001.

— *Promoting Health Through Public Policy*, Health Education Bureau, Dublin, 1987.

— *Quality and Fairness, A Health System for You*, Stationery Office, Dublin, 2001.

— *Report of Dr Deirdre Madden on Post Mortem Practice and Procedures*, Stationery Office, Dublin, 2006.

— *Report of the Advisory Body on Voluntary Health Insurance Scheme*, Stationery Office, Dublin, 1956.

— *Report of the Commission of Inquiry on Mental Illness*, Stationery Office, Dublin, 1966.

— *Report of the Commission on Health Funding*, Stationery Office, Dublin, 1989.

— *Report of the Commission on Nursing: A blueprint for the future*, Stationery Office, Dublin, 1998.
— *Report of the National Task Force on Medical Staffing* (*Hanly Report*), Stationery Office, Dublin, 2003.
— *Report of the Tribunal of Inquiry into the Blood Transfusion Service Board*, Stationery Office, Dublin, 1997.
— *Report of the Tribunal of Inquiry into the Infection with* HIV *and Hepatitis C of Persons with Haemophilia and Related Matters*, Stationery Office, Dublin, 2002.
— Robins, J. (ed.), *Reflections on Health: Commemorating Fifty Years of the Department of Health 1947–1997*, Department of Health, Dublin, 1997.
— Royal Commission on the Poor Laws and the Relief of Distress, *Report on Ireland*, 1909.
— Ryan, Annie, *Walls of Silence*, Red Lion Press, Kilkenny, 1999.
— *Shaping a Healthier Future*, Stationery Office, Dublin, 1994.
— *Strategic Task Force on Alcohol: Interim Report*, Department of Health and Children, 2002.
— Taylor, Desmond, *The Voluntary Health Insurance Board: The First Forty Years 1957–1997*, unpublished, 1997.
— *The Future Organisation of General Practice in Ireland: A Discussion Document*, Irish College of General Practitioners, Dublin, 1986.
— *The Health Services and their Further Development*, Stationery Office, Dublin, 1966.
— The Hospitals Commission, *First General Report*, Stationery Office, Dublin, 1936.
— *The Lourdes Hospital Inquiry*, Stationery Office, Dublin, 2006.
— *The Psychiatric Services: Planning for the Future*, Stationery Office, Dublin, 1984.
— *The Years Ahead: Policy for the Elderly*, Stationery Office, Dublin, 1988.
— *The Years Ahead Report: A Review of the Implementation of its Recommendations*, National Council on Ageing and Older People, Dublin, 1997.

— *Towards an Independent Future: Report of the Review Group on Health and Personal Social Services for People with Physical and Sensory Disabilities*, Stationery Office, Dublin, 1996.

— *Training and Employing the Handicapped: Report of a Working Party Established by the Minister for Health*, Stationery Office, Dublin, 1975.

— *Value for Money Audit of the Irish Health System, Main Report*, Deloitte & Touche in conjunction with the York Health Economics Consortium, Stationery Office, Dublin, 2001.

— Viney, Michael, *Growing Old in Ireland: The Irish Times Articles*, The Irish Times, Dublin, 1967.

— Walsh, Dermot, 'Mental Healthcare in Ireland 1945–1997 and the Future', in *Reflections on Health: Commemorating Fifty Years of the Department of Health 1947–1997*, Robins, J. (ed.), Department of Health, Dublin, 1997.

— *White Paper on Mental Health*, Stationery Office, Dublin, 1995.

— *White Paper: Outline of Proposals for the Improvement of the Health Services*, Stationery Office, Dublin, 1947.

— *White Paper: Private Health Insurance*, Stationery Office, Dublin, 1999.

— *White Paper: The Health Services and their Further Development*, Stationery Office, Dublin, 1966.

— Wiley, Miriam, 'Financing the Irish Health Services', in *Reflections on Health: Commemorating Fifty Years of the Department of Health 1947–1997*, Robins, J. (ed.), Department of Health, Dublin, 1997.

INDEX